estherpress

Books for Courageous Women

ESTHER PRESS VISION

Publishing diverse voices that encourage and equip women to walk courageously in the light of God's truth for such a time as this.

BIBLICAL STATEMENT OF PURPOSE

"For if you keep silent at this time, relief and deliverance will rise for the Jews from another place, but you and your father's house will perish. And who knows whether you have not come to the kingdom for such a time as this?"

Esther 4:14 (ESV)

What people are saying about …

DO THE THING

"*Do the Thing* delivers on its promise to bring gospel-centered goals, gumption, and grace for the go-getter girl. God has unique plans for all his daughters, and Rebecca beautifully helps us follow His lead and do the thing he calls us to. Every woman should read this book. I love it!"

Alli Worthington, speaker, coach, author of *Standing Strong*

"If you are a woman who wants to walk out her calling in confidence—doing it in a way that makes much of Jesus instead of elevating self—then this is the book for you! Rebecca George has crafted an insightful and biblical guide for discovering how to find your lane while honoring God and fulfilling your place in His kingdom. *Do the Thing* will equip you to cease striving, halt the comparisons, and finally become uniquely you. I wish my go-getter self had read this grace-filled gem a few decades ago!"

Karen Ehman, *New York Times* bestselling author, Proverbs 31 Ministries speaker, and Bible teacher in the *First 5* app

"When I met Rebecca a few years ago at a writer's conference, I knew there was something special and authentic about her. She had a gift deep inside her to cultivate community and conversations, and I knew I'd see this amazing woman do incredible things. This book—it's the real deal. Rebecca invites the reader close to her life, her struggles, her victories, and everything in-between. She challenges you to walk closer to Jesus while chasing down what He's assigned you to do. This book is a must-read for every woman who has ever wondered if she has what it takes."

Nicki Koziarz, three-time bestselling author and speaker with Proverbs 31 Ministries

"*Warning:* If you want to continue to stay stuck, exhausted, overwhelmed, and not make any forward progress on the things you can't go a day without thinking about … then put down *Do the Thing* and slowly back away right now! That's because Rebecca George delivers us a reveille of a wake-up call in this practical, insightful, *beautiful* book. It is a powerhouse of wisdom wrapped in the warm hug of a good, trusted friend. Rebecca takes us by the shoulders, shakes us just enough to get our attention, looks us in the eye, and tells us the time is NOW. This is the field guide every Go-Getter Girl needs to run the long race in front of her with endurance. One of the best books of the year—I can't wait to gift it to all my friends!"

Mary Marantz, bestselling author of *Dirt* and *Slow Growth Equals Strong Roots,* host of *The Mary Marantz Show*

"Whatever God is calling you to, you don't have to do it alone! Rebecca George is an encouraging, insightful guide whose words will help you move forward with more faith and less fear. You're here for such a time as this—so is this truth-filled, trust-building book."

Holley Gerth, bestselling author of *The Powerful Purpose of Introverts*

"Rebecca gives us that best-friend pep talk we all need to get moving. *Do The Thing* shares the truth of God through empowering stories that encourage us to start well and endure in the faith. This book will motivate you to discover God's purpose, get your head in the game, and find the determination to do that thing! If you're looking for courage and confidence to step into God's game plan and do big things, this is the book for you!"

Jenny Randle, ministry leader, podcast host, and author of *Dream Come True*

"Jesus hasn't just saved you *from* something but *for* something—'the thing' you know God made you to do for His glory and the good of others. That's the heart of this gospel-centric book! I highly recommend it."

Jordan Raynor, bestselling author of *Redeeming Your Time* and *The Creator in You*

"Finally! A gospel-centered approach to tackling negative thoughts and challenges against our God-given callings. Rebecca gives the help, coaching, and push we Christian women need to do the thing God is leading us to do. Closed the book with a fist pump in the air, ready to take the next step!"

Heidi Anderson, author of *P.S. It's Gonna Be Good*, Christian influencer @heidileeanderson

"If you have an idea, a project, a dream, or a passion that you've felt unable to make progress on, *Do The Thing* is for you. Rebecca will not only show you how to clarify the thing—or glory goal—but also help you take practical steps toward pursuing it. She provides you with guidance as you navigate the many bumps, distractions, and challenges that will come as you pursue your thing."

Esther Littlefield, business coach; host of the *Christian Woman Leadership* podcast and *Christian Woman Business* podcast

REBECCA GEORGE

DO THE THING

GOSPEL-CENTERED GOALS, GUMPTION, AND GRACE FOR THE GO-GETTER GIRL

e℗
estherpress

Books for Courageous Women
from David C Cook

DO THE THING
Published by Esther Press,
An imprint of David C Cook
4050 Lee Vance Drive
Colorado Springs, CO 80918 U.S.A.

Integrity Music Limited, a Division of David C Cook
Brighton, East Sussex BN1 2RE, England

ISBN 978-0-8307-8435-6
eISBN 978-0-8307-8436-3

The Team: Susan McPherson, Stephanie Bennett, Julie Cantrell, Judy
Gillispie, Karissa Silvers, James Hershberger, Susan Murdock
Cover Design: James Hershberger
Cover Photo: Getty Images

Printed in the United States of America
First Edition 2023

1 2 3 4 5 6 7 8 9 10

120922

To Danielle, the friend who came, stayed, and cheered louder for me than I could ever deserve. This book is in the world, in part, because God used your encouragement to help me not quit for the last eight years. Thank you ... Love you big.

CONTENTS

Foreword by Michelle Myers   13

Introduction   17

Chapter 1: Heaven on Our Hearts   23

Chapter 2: The Freedom of a Blank Canvas   43

Chapter 3: Spirit-Led Stick-to-itiveness   63

Chapter 4: Own the Ordinary   79

Chapter 5: The Genesis of Striving   93

Chapter 6: The Invitation to a Finished Work   109

Chapter 7: Illuminate the Talent around You   125

Chapter 8: The Tension of Time   141

Chapter 9: Interrupt the Overwhelm   159

Chapter 10: Silence the Critic   177

Chapter 11: Lay Down the Measuring Stick   197

Chapter 12: Fall in Love with Your Lane   213

Here's What I Hope   229

Acknowledgments   231

Notes   233

FOREWORD

I actually met Rebecca in one of the "do the thing" moments of my life. My best friend and ministry partner, Somer Phoebus, and I had just turned in the completed manuscript for *She Works His Way*, the book that tells the story and mission of the work we've been in the trenches doing for the last decade. When our publisher told us our first podcast interview to promote the book was scheduled with Rebecca, even though we'd had thousands of conversations like this one, I had bats (*way beyond butterflies!*) in my stomach. It felt like the ministry version of a blind date ... that would be *recorded*.

But the moment Rebecca popped up on Zoom, she greeted us with a huge smile, showered us with encouragement, and put us at ease—not just for our conversation with her but for all the conversations that followed.

I have no doubt you'll sense that same spirit as you read her words.

Rebecca has been living this message out long before she ever planned to write this book. You'll learn quickly that she believes God wholeheartedly and takes Him at His word—and because of that, she knows that believing Him for ourselves is only where our walk with the Lord begins.

As we grow in grace and our knowledge of Him, we keep taking faith steps, one of those steps being to help others believe in God and take their own steps of obedience.

And that's why you're here right now: not to become a superfan of Rebecca (*even though you will seriously adore her!*) or to simply spike your productivity level. Her entire reason for writing this is to equip you to put Proverbs 3:5–6 into practice: to trust God with all your heart, refusing to lean on your own understanding, so you will *acknowledge Him* in everything you *do.*

That's a familiar passage, so if you glossed over it, take a deep breath and ask God to help you see the truth that's written there with fresh eyes. It's easy to say we trust God with all our hearts, but it's much harder to throw self-doubt and self-sufficiency out the window so that everything we do will acknowledge *Him*, not ourselves.

But here's the really, *really* good news—what you, me, and Rebecca all have in common: we don't have to do this alone, and we don't have to rely on our own strength to make it happen. Second Corinthians 12:9 reminds us: "My grace is sufficient for you, for my power is made perfect in weakness."

If you'll bring your weakness and your willingness to God, that's all He needs to empower you to do the thing.

That's why I'm so excited you're here reading this right now. This is not just a textbook that helps you gain knowledge but a workbook that helps you take inventory, then a guidebook that helps you take action. Rebecca is not only incredibly personal, sharing both Scripture that instructs and stories that illustrate, but she effortlessly weaves from the foundational to the practical. And I mean it when I tell you, she really cares about you and she genuinely believes in you.

But Michelle, how can she believe in me when she doesn't even know me?

Because she knows your God. And that's all she needs to know to be 100 percent confident that if your yes is on the table for Him to use, then there's no limit to what He can do through you.

Let me leave you with three lessons God has repeatedly shown me as I've done the thing:

1. **God is not small, so nothing He asks you to do is small either.** The significance of your assignment is not wrapped up in the size of the task but the size of the One who gave it.

2. **Don't get hung up waiting on a specific assignment.** God calls all His children to three general tasks: to make disciples (see Matt. 28:19–20), to love God, and to love others (see 22:37–39). Get involved in God's general work in the world by taking these assignments seriously, and there He will show you the thing you're called to do.

3. **God's assignments often come in people form.** And ironically enough, the more purposeful the work, the easier it is to stop prioritizing people. Consider David, who received God's vision for the temple but wasn't tasked with building it. David's role was to build Solomon so Solomon could build the temple (see 1 Kings 7–8). As you do the thing, focus on *who* you build for the kingdom, not just *what* you build for the kingdom.

God, do more than we could ask or imagine with our weakness and willingness. Give us the grace and courage we need to do the thing. We love You, and we trust You. In Jesus' name, amen.

Michelle Myers
author of She Works His Way *and the*
Conversational Commentary series

INTRODUCTION

Do you have a "thing"—a special cause, project, or talent that you feel called to do? Maybe you're already doing your "thing," or maybe God is shifting you in a new direction. Either way, do the steps He's asking you to take feel a little too uncertain? Or maybe a *lot* too scary? Do you sometimes feel overwhelmed by the choices you're facing? Or ill-equipped to live the life you were born to live?

If you answered yes to any (or all) of these questions, I understand your struggle because I've been there too.

When it comes to attacking, the Enemy is not very innovative. Oftentimes, he comes for us with a subtle question (much as he did to Eve in Gen. 3:1). *Did God really say that? Did He really create you to use your voice, skills, gifts, or talents? Does He really want you to grow, learn, or lead in that way?* If the Enemy can get a foothold in our minds, making us doubt God's Word, then he can gain some ground that he was never meant to hold.

The truth is, you are gifted by God in a unique way. Yes, YOU!

No one has been wired with the exact measure of gift, skill, and wisdom that God has lavished on your life. *You matter,* my friend. And if you ever start to doubt that truth, remember that the Creator of the universe has planted you exactly where you are right now and has equipped you with everything you need to complete the journey ahead. A journey He has planned JUST. FOR. YOU!

Perhaps you have a full-time job but you find yourself oozing with passion for a certain creative outlet. Maybe you're a stay-at-home mom who longs to lead a new ministry, volunteer project, or nonprofit. Or maybe you're an entrepreneur who is yearning to launch a new business, farmstead, or co-op.

While I don't know exactly what brought you to this book, I do know you're here for a reason. And I suspect you want to discover how God desires to use *your* time here on earth to make Him known.

No one has been wired with the exact measure of gift, skill, and wisdom that God has lavished on your life.

We all know God does not *need* us to accomplish His agenda, but what an unmerited gift that He *chooses* to use us to bring His light to the world. Let's not waste another minute of this all-too-brief time we have on this side of eternity. Instead, let's navigate these murky waters together, using His Word as our compass as we "do the thing" God has designed for each of us to do.

My prayer is that when you're finished with this book, the pages will be dog-eared, tattered, worn, and full of highlights—not because of the words I've written but because God is using His infallible, ever-present Word to *change our hearts*. I'm trusting that through the lens of His truth, He'll help us see ourselves as He sees us. And that He'll give us **the goals, gumption, and grace** we need to become the **go-getter girls** He created us to be.

Let's Go, Girls!

Goodness, how I wish we were seated across from each other at a dimly lit coffee shop, where I could hear your heart, learn your story, and find out exactly what led you to this message. I'd have a lavender-honey latte in hand, and the floors would creak beneath our chairs as we slowly dived deep into conversation about our dreams and our fears.

While I can't be with you in person, you can certainly explore this book as an individual reader. Yet I encourage you to invite at least one friend to share this experience with you because we truly are better together (no matter what your drink of choice might be).

Take my dear friend Danielle, for example. We met in college more than a decade ago, and she's still a spunky, creative soul with a heart so full of Jesus it could burst. Even in seasons when countries separated us, we wrote letters back and forth to each other, always making our friendship a priority. Now we live eight hours apart. So when we do get the chance to meet, we plan for at least a three-hour date, during which we talk about what God is doing in our lives.

That's what I hope this book feels like to you. *I want to be your Danielle.* I want to be that person you know is 100 percent on your side no matter how far apart we may be. I want to offer you that safe, calm space where you feel free to open your heart and explore the questions that stir your soul.

Throughout this book:

- Each chapter will explore potential challenges or obstacles we may face when called to "do the thing." We'll turn to Scripture for specific examples that point us back to Jesus, and you'll find prompts to help you bring your hopes, dreams, and concerns to God in prayer.

- The end of each chapter provides a section called "**For the Go-Getter Girl**." Here, you will explore how God is speaking specifically to *you*. We'll revisit key takeaways and examine areas where God might be prompting you to take action. You may complete these activities by writing directly inside the book, or you may prefer to grab a journal and write more about certain topics.

- With each chapter, you'll discover a new statement to be added to the "**Do the Thing Manifesto**." I encourage you to read this aloud or share it with a friend as you move forward. This exercise gives us words to stand on when we need encouragement.

- You'll also find six accompanying **videos** in which I will guide you through specific action steps to help you "do the thing." This video content is free to you and can be viewed alone or with a group. Access the videos by visiting the link or scanning the QR code on the next page.

As we take this journey together, we will discover how to:

1. See our gifts and talents from a **gospel**-centered perspective.
2. Prioritize **goals** that matter most as we move forward with **gumption** and **grace**.
3. Overcome negative thought patterns related to our callings so we can work and create with the confidence of a **go-getter girl**!

Let's walk in the freedom we have in Christ and *do the thing* together. In the famous words of my favorite nineties icon Shania Twain, "Let's go, girls!"

Access the Videos Here
https://davidccook.org/
prd/do-the-thing
Access code: **DoTheThing**
Or scan the QR code:

Chapter 1

HEAVEN ON OUR HEARTS

A few years ago, as I trained for the St. Jude Memphis Marathon, I had some big goals in mind. I was hoping to beat my personal record of 4:25 and run the 26.2-mile course in under four hours. Fighting the extreme heat and humidity, I ran stride for stride with my best running buddy, Kristi—until around mile 12. At that point, her gait remained smooth as she focused on finishing strong. Despite my best efforts, she eventually pulled ahead of me, and I had to face the hard truth that I was *not* going to meet my desired time.

As partners, Kristi and I had agreed that we would never hold each other back, so I cheered for her as my own goal slipped through my hands.

By mile 13, I had already passed through the St. Jude campus, where patients and their families lined the streets to encourage the runners. I cried (I always do!) and pushed through what I *thought* would be the most emotional part of the race. But as I entered the last 10K, God did something special.

With heat exhaustion and personal frustration setting in, I was tempted to call it quits. Then, as I approached a downtown bridge, a little girl in a wheelchair caught my attention. Perhaps reading my name on my bib, she and her family started cheering, "Go, Rebecca. Go!" Their voices lifted my spirits and, suddenly, I could breathe easier. But it wasn't just their cheers that inspired me. This girl was holding a sign that read: "The same power that raised Jesus from the grave is living inside you. YOU CAN DO THIS!"

If we actively partner with God, He will empower us by His strength to serve Him and love others.

Tears streamed down my face as I was reminded that the Holy Spirit was alive *inside me*. Did I still have to do the hard work of putting one foot in front of the other to reach the finish line? You bet. However, for the remaining 6.2 miles, the words on her sign echoed in my mind, fueling me forward until I collapsed into Kristi's arms. (She had finished about five minutes before me.)

Isn't that race experience like our walk with Jesus? We get weary. Something happens to remind us that He is sufficient and that we simply cannot do anything without Him. Then, once we remember the Divine is taking up residence inside us and we are never alone, we hold tight to our faith and finish the work we are called to do.

For me, running a marathon is always a great reminder that I have limits and God does not. In endurance running, we don't race the clock. We race the distance. In other words, it's not the time that crushes us mentally, physically, and emotionally; it's the number of miles we must endure to cross the finish line.

Like a marathon, a spiritual journey is a long game. No matter how defeated we may feel, we have to keep putting one foot in front of the other and never give up.

You might be feeling like you don't have what it takes to start that business, train for that triathlon, or lead that small group. The simple truth is this: you don't. But in Christ, you DO! That's the secret. If we actively partner with God, He will empower us by His strength to serve Him and love others (see Rom. 8:11).

I tell you all this not to suggest you go sign up for a marathon (although I'd love for everyone to experience the thrill of crossing that finish line). Rather, I tell you this story because, as you dare to do the thing God is calling you to do, you may have moments of exhaustion and personal frustration along the way. You may even have moments when you want to call it quits. In those difficult stretches, I hope you'll picture me cheering you forward, shouting "Go, friend. Go!" Page by page, I'll be right here by your side, holding up a sign that reads: "The same power that raised Jesus from the grave is living inside you. YOU CAN DO THIS!"

Find Your Foundation

Since we're talking about marathons, something else I've learned as a long-distance runner is that I need to wear the right shoes in the race. And because I'm not trained as a cross-country runner, it also helps for me to run on a solid surface rather than a rugged trail. Likewise, to move forward in our spiritual journeys, we must start with the right foundation.

Are you familiar with the bestselling novel *Redeeming Love* by Francine Rivers? If so, you may remember that the first fifty pages (!) make up the prologue. I confess, I nervously wondered if I would ever get through that first chunk of *Redeeming Love*. But had I skipped the prologue, I would have missed the fullness of the story that Francine so beautifully penned for us.

Recently I was honored to interview Francine for my podcast (a dream!). During the conversation, she shared that she hoped readers would not skip the prologue in her novel, for it is vital to understanding the rest of the book. In other words, if readers didn't anchor themselves firmly to that foundation first, the rest of the story wouldn't make much sense.

The same is true for us in life. We must begin with seeing ourselves as God (our Author) sees us. Only then will we understand the full journey He has called us to take.

A Kingdom Perspective

Although we each carry out different jobs here on earth, God created us all to glorify Him through worship and through our work. While that may sound simple, this mission may prove difficult at times.

Why?

Because we live in a fallen world.

As Christians, we long for Eden, for the return of what this world was designed to be: faithful people living in perfect fellowship and communion with our Creator. This fellowship was broken as soon as Adam and Eve partook of the forbidden fruit, shame entered the picture, and "fig-leaf religion" (as A. W. Tozer called it) came on the scene. In his book, *The Purpose of Man*, Tozer writes, Adam and Eve "lost the focus of their inward beauty and purpose, and no longer satisfied the criteria of fellowship with their Creator."[1]

Adam and Eve's story teaches us that we can't afford to lose our focus on our inward beauty and God-given purpose. Nor can we lose fellowship with our Creator.

In my early twenties, I was waiting on a lot of dreams to come true. I believed God had gifted me to write and to speak, but was discipling a group of college girls in my living room enough? I believed He wanted me to be a wife, but were any of my dates ever going to lead me to the right husband? I cared deeply about being a good friend, but how many bridal showers and engagement parties could I plan for everyone else while my dates kept resulting in dead ends?

Feeling weary, I sat in church one morning desperately needing a dose of hope. Loneliness and self-doubt cut deep that day. Then we sang "King of My Heart."

> *Let the King of my heart be*
> *The mountain where I run*
> *The fountain I drink from …*
> *He is my song.[2]*

As the chorus swelled, I began to doubt the message: "You're never gonna let me down." I began praying and telling God how I really felt: *let down* by my life circumstances. That's when the Holy Spirit spoke to me and asked, "Rebecca, who do you know that I am?"

I mentally began listing off everything I knew to be true about God: He is sufficient, all-knowing, faithful, omnipresent, a provider, a sustainer, a deliverer …

And you know what I realized? These aspects of His character were truer than true and could never be compromised. While life might have let me down in that season, God had not. Suddenly, 2 Timothy 2:13 had a whole new meaning for me: "If we are faithless, he remains faithful—for he cannot deny himself." In other words, God's faithfulness didn't hinge on my ability to notice it in that season of disappointment.

Because of the brokenness we experience in this world, it's easy to become discouraged, burned out, and even cynical about the path we've been given. When we lose sight of eternity, we can end up chasing quick wins and temporal rewards. Whether we find short bursts of relief from shopping, skydiving, exercising, or the like, those dopamine hits will soon fade, leaving us looking for our next easy "high."

But with *heaven on our hearts*, we can lay aside the temporary for the eternal.

Hebrews 12:1–2 reminds us to "lay aside every weight, and sin which clings so closely, and let us run with endurance the race that is set before us, looking to Jesus, the founder and perfecter of our faith." As directed in these verses, we must make a daily choice to surrender to the obedience of Christ as we pursue the tasks He has placed before us.

Knowing I am made to worship a sufficient and all-knowing God, I want to make choices in alignment with what I know to be true about Him. Perhaps you've lost sight of God's character in your current season. Maybe you *have* taken steps to do the thing, but you haven't quite seen the progress you anticipated.

If you came to this chapter feeling weary today, as if life has let *you* down, remember that God's character remains, always. And He is bringing everything together for your good … in His divine timing.

You Have a Helper

One risk as a runner is that you can get a little too excited, a little too self-confident, and charge ahead on all cylinders right out of the gate. Needless to say, that kind of *overstriving* can lead to burning out before you ever reach the goal. The same can be said about the work God has called us to do. We may embark on that "race" with great magnitude, believing that if we can just work hard enough, run fast enough, hustle long enough, then we can do the thing and give God all the glory.

The problem is that we learned this way of thinking from the world, not from Him.

We cannot accomplish God's will for our lives by ourselves, no matter how much we strive. That's a rat race we were never created to run. The truth is, we don't have to work harder, run faster, or hustle longer to give God all the glory (nor do we do any of these things to earn His love). Rather, we move forward at the healthy pace He designed us to move at and stay the course. Jesus promises the Holy Spirit as a "Helper" who will empower us as we share the gospel with others (John 15:26).

You have His power coursing through your veins, filling in the cracks of your weaknesses so that He may be glorified.

Maybe you own a small business and can honor God by the way you treat your customers. Perhaps you are a ministry leader fully relying on God as you prepare to speak at a conference. Or you may be a stay-at-home mom feeling led to tutor in your few minutes of spare time.

I don't know your story, but I do know that as a follower of Jesus, you have a helper in the Holy Spirit. You have His power coursing through your veins, filling in the cracks of your weaknesses so that He may be glorified.

Some people resist a deep dependence on God because that kind of surrender means admitting weakness. It can be scary to admit our own limitations. But personally, I shudder at the thought of a life without the power of Christ guiding my work. Your greatest ideas, your most brilliant endeavors, will be a by-product of you partnering with the King of the Universe.

As Paul tells us in 2 Corinthians 12:9–10, "[God] said to me, 'My grace is sufficient for you, for my power is made perfect in weakness.' Therefore, I will boast all the more gladly of my weaknesses, so that the power of Christ may rest upon me. For the sake of Christ, then, I am content with weaknesses, insults, hardships, persecutions, and calamities. For when I am weak, then I am strong."

The more aware I am of my weaknesses, the more awake I am to God's power in my life. If we could all become better "weakness braggers," then I think we could all live with a deeper dependence on Christ in our everyday lives.

Flip the Lights On

After I graduated from the University of Tennessee, I scored my first "big girl" job—an HR role that was a little bit of a catchall. On any given day I could be leading a new-hire orientation, completing verifications of employment, or conducting interviews. At twenty-two years old, I had figured out that I loved serving people. But I didn't quite know how to balance my deep love for Jesus with the gifts and talents I was beginning to see develop in my life. Even then I was a little too opinionated and spunky for ministry (as it had been modeled for me), and I really, really, really liked Shania Twain's music. Do you see the dichotomy here? I wanted something more than corporate America, but I also felt I didn't fit the mold of "ministry leader" as I knew it. (The irony that I went on to marry a pastor is not lost on me.)

I loved encouraging others, especially women, and I was beginning to recognize my gifts for writing, speaking, and leading. But I had no idea how I was supposed to use those passions to serve God.

Can you relate?

I desperately wanted to find the assignment God had for me. Little did I know, I was exactly where He wanted me to be. I failed to see that I could make God known through the ordinary moments of my normal routine.

How often do we walk right past the doors God puts before us? Maybe you don't like grading papers as a teacher. But by investing in the hearts of children, you could be changing the course of their eternity. Or perhaps you don't like the administrative paperwork you must complete for a specific project. But what if that paperwork could earn the grant needed to put your faith in action for people in need?

I've found that God uses my gifts in many different spheres of my life. It's okay (actually, it's amazing!) to find ways to use your gifts outside the local church. We must look outside ourselves to see ways we can serve where we are, here and now.

Perhaps Martin Luther King Jr. said it best:

> And when you discover what you will be in your life, set out to do it as if God Almighty called you at this particular moment in history to do it. Don't just set out to do a good job. Set out to do such a good job that the living, the dead or the unborn couldn't do it any better.
>
> If it falls your lot to be a street sweeper, sweep streets like Michelangelo painted pictures, sweep streets like Beethoven composed music, sweep streets like Leontyne Price sings before the Metropolitan Opera. Sweep streets like Shakespeare wrote poetry. Sweep streets so well that all the hosts of heaven and earth will have to pause and say: Here lived a great street sweeper who swept his job well.[3]

When that light switch of understanding is turned on, the connection between our gifts and His glory is made. As 1 Peter 4:10 says, "As each has received a gift, use it to serve one another, as good stewards of God's varied grace."

Keep your eyes up, sister. And sweep those streets with joy on your face, knowing you're working from a kingdom mindset with a deep dependence on the One who set you free.

Are you ready to flip on your light switch?

The Lampstand

One night as I brought macaroni to a boil over the stove, my husband, Dustin (who by now you know is a pastor), shared an analogy about how we can each think of ourselves as an oil lamp, usable by God when we surrender our desires to His will.

As you know, when it is lit, the wick in a lamp gives light to the area surrounding it. The wick, Dustin explained, represents our gifts and talents. Each of us has been given our own unique skills (or wicks). Some wicks are longer than others. Some are wider than others. Some burn faster than others. Some are more frayed than others. But they all serve the same purpose: to shine God's light into the darkness.

Still, the wick cannot burn without oil.

In Scripture, oil is often used to symbolize the Holy Spirit. Just as the oil in a lamp must be refilled, our spiritual "oil" must be replenished by walking in step with Christ, communing with God in prayer, and reading His Word daily.

Inspired by Dustin's perspective, I set the wooden spoon down on the stove. "Wow!" I said, "I've never thought about my life as a believer in that way!"

Later, as I was reading my Bible, I continued to unravel this theme of the oil lamp. In the Old Testament, the Lord instructed Moses on how to care for the lamps in the tabernacle, God's dwelling place. If we take a deeper look at God's words in Leviticus 24, we can apply those same instructions to our lives today:

Command the people of Israel to bring you pure oil from beaten olives for the lamp, that a light may be kept burning regularly. Outside the veil of the testimony, in the tent of meeting, Aaron shall arrange it from evening to morning before the LORD regularly. It shall be a statute forever throughout your generations. He shall arrange the lamps on the lampstand of pure gold before the LORD regularly. (vv. 2–4)

It's important to realize that these lamps were the light source inside the tabernacle. They were the very means by which people could experience the presence of God. Therefore, it was crucial to keep the oil replenished and the wicks trimmed so the light could continue to shine.

Why does this matter to us, now that Christ has been resurrected, enabling our bodies to serve as God's temple? What can we possibly learn from how the Israelites tended the lamps of the tabernacle?

Again, it's important to realize that oil is used a symbol of the Holy Spirit's presence. Though the Holy Spirit lives within us, we must keep the "oil" replenished if we hope to keep the Holy Spirit at the center of our lives.

The wicks of our lamps also need to be trimmed if we want God's light to continue shining through us. God accomplishes this by bringing us through trials, crossing our paths with various people, and even letting us experience deep suffering or loss in order that we might become more sanctified in the image of Jesus Christ. This can be a very painful process, but as followers of Jesus, we are not promised freedom from pain. *Quite the opposite.* Jesus promises us that we will experience sorrows, but He also reminds us that even our pain has a purpose.

Three times in Leviticus, we are told the lamps are to be tended to "regularly" or "continually." The same goes for us today.

It's important to recognize that when we burn the candle at both ends, striving for success or accolades or approval, we will quickly burn out and our oil will run dry. By keeping the Holy Spirit as our guide and allowing God to "trim" our lives to His will, we can serve as His vessels and allow the Light of the World to shine through us.

Who Cares?

I often coach other creatives who are hoping to begin a podcast or ministry that God has laid on their hearts. Recently our youth pastor, Kreig, came to me about a podcast idea that had been swirling around in his head. He nervously played with a straw wrapper on the table as he told me how he wanted to honor the important ministry leaders in his life. "I want their stories to be told," he said. "I know they'll never write books, but they are doing amazing things to further the gospel. I've learned so much from them, and I think others would too."

After going around and around with him about different ideas and strategies, I finally said, "Kreig, I think there's something you need to establish before you hit Record. Figure out how this project matters to you, how it matters to God, and how it's going to matter to other people."

Have you been wrestling with a big idea and don't know what to do next? If so, I offer the same advice.

First, discover why this project matters to you. That fire you feel deep inside is God-given. All you have to do is lean into those desires and discover how you can use that passion to further the kingdom.

Second, discover why this project matters to God. Remember, He has gone before you in this next season, and your calling was His idea long before you were even born. Praying and seeking His glory ensures that your work will honor Him and further the message of the gospel. This is how good ideas become great ideas.

Third, discover why it matters to other people. Some business ideas fail simply because they don't have their end consumer in mind. Blockbuster eventually tanked because technology advanced far beyond its vision of the future. After years of success, Toys"R"Us flopped due to the growth of online retailers, which made it easier for customers to shop without needing to visit a brick-and-mortar store. We must ensure we're cultivating an idea that serves the specific needs of the people we are trying to reach, and we must be willing to shift that service appropriately as their needs change over time.

Glory Goals

As A. W. Tozer wrote in *The Purpose of Man*, our purpose is "that we might worship God and enjoy Him forever."[4] God's glory should be our ultimate aim. Our pursuits should be an act of worship. The way we love others should give evidence of our surrender to Christ. The tasks we pour ourselves into should be done with such care, responsibility, and grace that they make a nonbeliever stop and wonder who we're living for.

In a recent worship service, before my husband stood to preach, we sang "Evermore," a very popular song by Jason Breland. I had been writing this chapter, and the lyrics led me to pray that you, too, could enjoy God through worshipping Him. As you think about what God is whispering in your heart, I encourage you to pray these words:

> *Evermore I will love You, evermore I will serve You*
> *Evermore I will glorify the name of the Lord*

Evermore I'll adore You, evermore bow before You
I will bless Your name forevermore.[5]

I think we all can become overwhelmed by the idea of a "purpose" or "calling." We're sent mixed messages by the world as to what "success" means (and how to achieve it). It's easy to become so focused on the negatives that we become paralyzed by fear (another clever ploy of the Enemy).

That's why we're going to change up our language to gain a clearer picture of where God is leading each of us. Let's start by calling this "thing" our *glory goal*.

What do I mean by a glory goal? A **glory goal** is our attempt to clearly communicate our faith through our actions: "This is how I am using my gifts and talents to advance the kingdom and bring God glory." It is the God-given assignment that will allow us to further the gospel and make disciples along the way.

Your glory goal might seem small, or it might seem larger than life. No matter what it is, your glory goal will require surrender. As you move to a complete dependence on God and walk in step with the Holy Spirit, you'll develop a "more of Him, less of me" mentality, remembering the declaration: "You have the same power that raised Jesus from the grave living inside you. YOU CAN DO THIS."

When we live in this truth, we are able to work from a place of gospel-centered, here-to-worship-God purpose. *This* is where glory goals are born.

Discovering Your Thing

What were you made for? This is one of the most important questions you'll ever answer about your life. Perhaps your path is unclear and you're wondering,

Well, what does this "do the thing" idea really look like in my life? What is my glory goal?

To answer these questions, I encourage you to think about where you are naturally gifted. For example, while some people may find organizing closets stressful, you might find it therapeutic. If so, maybe God has gifted you with organizational skills. Perhaps you have a knack for tackling spreadsheets or tracking your family's budget and finances. Maybe planning busy schedules, leading meetings, or managing travel is your thing.

Whether it's sewing, baking, cleaning, or couponing, your interests and passions can be considered sacred work, especially when you use your talents not to gain praise from others but to shout praises in adoration of the King.

It might take some prayer and thought to discover your God-given talent, but this important discovery will give you clarity as you move forward.

Prayer Prompts

Use these prayer prompts to help you pray and journal about what God is revealing to you in this chapter.

God, will You help me:

- see how I can use my gifts and talents to honor You in this season

- determine what my glory goal might be

- live like the Holy Spirit is taking up residence inside me

FOR THE GO-GETTER GIRL

SCRIPTURE FOR REFLECTION

- 2 Corinthians 12:1–10
- Ephesians 2:1–10
- Hebrews 12:1–2

GOALS

Remember creating Venn diagrams in school? Typically, these are used to chart similarities and differences between certain things. Let's use this compare-contrast technique to help you discover your calling. Here's a quick personal example.

DISCOVER MY CALLING

What matters to you?
Writing, speaking, leading women

MY CALLING
Author

The message of the gospel

Encouragement, wisdom, instruction

What matters to God?

What matters to other people?

Using the **Discover My Calling Venn Diagram** that follows, let's chart the intersection of what matters to *you*, what matters to *God*, and what matters to *other people*.

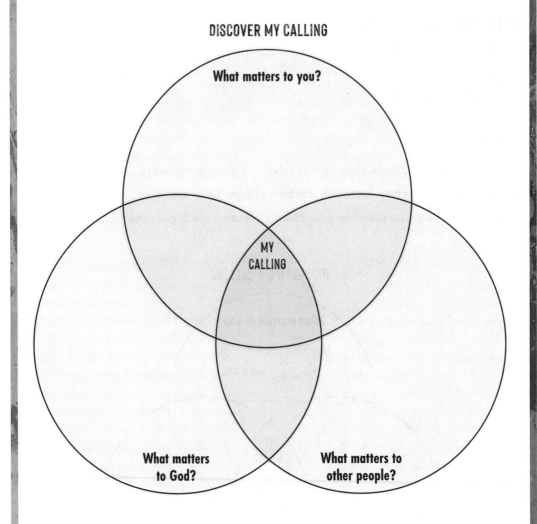

DISCOVER MY CALLING

What matters to you?

MY
CALLING

What matters
to God?

What matters to
other people?

GUMPTION

• What does the analogy of the oil lamp teach us about our need to partner with God?

GRACE

• As a follower of Jesus Christ, you are not dependent on your own strength. You have the same power that raised Jesus from the grave living inside you. What would it look like to rely on God's power in you when you're feeling weak?

DO THE THING MANIFESTO

Review our manifesto statement for chapter 1. Depending on your learning style, you may want to write it down, share it with a friend, or read the words aloud.

I am a go-getter girl for the kingdom of God. I seek to make Jesus Christ known through my work and to live in dependence on Him as I use my gifts and talents.

Chapter 2

THE FREEDOM OF A BLANK CANVAS

Larry Ladd, otherwise known as my papaw, is a true artist, craftsman, and historian. A retired engineer, he's one of the most creative minds I've ever known. A wooden necklace organizer and jewelry box are just a few of the many creations he's brought to life through the years, and he built the kitchen table I'll take to my grave. I'm thankful to be in the lineage of his creativity, much of which he passed on to my mom, who then passed it on to me.

One day, Papaw called me with an excited tone in his voice. "Hey, Rebecca," he said. "I found an oil painting class. Would you be interested in taking it with me?"

Of course, I quickly said yes. What kind of granddaughter would pass up an opportunity to share such special time with her beloved papaw?

A few weeks later, off we went to a Hobby Lobby not too far from my grandparents' home—a beautiful spread of farmland nestled in the foothills of the Smokies. Together, Papaw and I walked into the well-lit classroom, where small canvases and palettes of colorful oil paint had been carefully arranged. We had signed up to paint a wintery lake and its surrounding mountain terrain. The picture online was gorgeous, but as I studied the example displayed at the front of the class, my jaw dropped. How would we complete such a masterpiece in only a few hours?

Determined to see this activity through, we each chose a workstation and settled in. In my opinion, the teacher had not poured nearly enough colors of paint into our palettes, and I had no idea how we would ever leave with a finished product that resembled anything close to the display.

The lead instructor, Nick, introduced himself and gave us a quick rundown of how to use our supplies. My mind spun as I tried to act like I knew what I was doing. In front of me: a blank canvas. It was full of possibility, but fear and insecurity began to well up in my heart, just as they do when I begin any new endeavor. *What if I'm bad at this? What if Nick works too quickly? What if I don't understand the techniques and I totally screw this up?*

Because Papaw had already paid for the course, quitting was not an option. I took a deep breath, wet my brushes, and listened closely to Nick's instruction as my beloved grandfather and I began our creative journey together.

You know what I discovered?

Those first brush strokes across the canvas were the scariest.

The more I trusted Nick's guidance, the more freedom I felt to paint my own canvas. Stroke by stroke, a beautiful creation began to come together. It took time, intentionality, and a big ol' dose of courage, but as we mixed the colors into different hues and utilized various brush strokes, I slowly realized I'd been given absolutely everything I needed to be successful.

During the lunch break, Papaw and I discussed our strategy for the second half of the class. We laughed at our own insecurities, acknowledging that we had come a long way since that morning and agreeing that once we got going, our confidence had been boosted.

The big lesson? There wasn't much that was unfixable.

We learned that oil paint doesn't dry immediately, so almost any mistake could be worked out. No misstep was wasted that day. Rather, every stroke became part of the finished product, should we choose to see it that way.

Hours later, with sore necks and shoulder muscles, Papaw and I were both proud of what we'd accomplished. Our paintings uniquely represented our individual creativity and were both beautiful in their own right—his trees a little more precise than mine and my water's edge a little more pronounced. We had both been given the same measure of paint to work with and the same instructions, but it's what we did with that opportunity that made the difference.

As I scanned the various participants in the room, I realized that our paintings were representative of so much more than oil on a canvas. They were a symbol of what happens in our lives when we pursue our passions to the glory of God.

Many times, we think we don't have the skills or equipment we need. It's easy to look around at what others are doing and feel as if we're not good enough. When we don't know the next step, we can panic, assuming we'll fail and forgetting we have a leader there to guide us to our end goal.

We each have been given the exact equipment and skills we need to complete a life of faithfulness. Our offering may look different from other people's, but that's all part of the fun as we honor God's unique desires for us. If we dare to trust our Teacher and walk step by step with Him, He will mold our talents into something beautiful that will bring glory to His name.

Say It Out Loud

Dreaming about what God is inviting us to create feels exciting. It's a lot like approaching a blank canvas, isn't it? The space between what isn't and what could be. Sometimes we struggle to get started not because we don't know what God is inviting us into but because we're not relying on the Holy Spirit to actually do the thing. We can hesitate in fear instead of taking steps forward in faith.

A few years ago, I had to navigate my own blank canvas.

My heart was pounding as I sat at a pizza place in Knoxville, Tennessee, where my friend Gen had promised to meet me. Trying not to watch the clock, I sprinkled salt on the napkin under my glass of Diet Coke so it wouldn't sweat through. Just then, Gen texted. "Stuck in traffic … be there soon!" Minute by minute, I was growing increasingly restless as I wrestled with that Holy Spirit gut check that happens when He calls you to move, to stand, or to start something bigger than yourself but you don't feel ready. Do you know that feeling?

Outside, the weather was cold. Tennessee cold. Cold-to-the-bone cold. And, to be honest, that's exactly how I had been feeling about my life. This season had been intense. For one thing, my mom had been going through treatments for breast cancer. (Praise God, she beat it seven years ago.) With the stressors adding up, I had traded a mountaintop season of successfully "adulting" for a season in the valley, leaning hard on Jesus with every new day—or if I'm being honest, every breath.

I had been incredibly blessed with a job I liked, a community I adored, a family I loved, and yet, there was that c word, hanging over it all like a big dark storm ruining a beautiful garden party. No amount of "good" in my life could erase the fact that my mom had cancer. It didn't help that I was living an hour and a half away from her as she underwent major surgery, chemotherapy, and radiation. Maybe that's why my heart had been feeling stirred to encourage other people who were facing that icky, yucky, painful c word.

As I drifted away in thought, Gen danced over to the table and enveloped me in a big bear hug. She quickly took her seat opposite me in the booth, and we picked right back up where we had last left off. (If you've ever had a close girlfriend, you get it.) Eventually, the conversation drifted to my mom. "How is she?" Gen asked. I went on to tell her about the good days and the bad, the struggles of living so close yet so far away, and how much I longed to see the other side of the healing journey that was just beginning.

We laughed and cried together. As I was struggling with how to be a good daughter, friend, and coworker during this challenging season, I had to check my emotions on a moment-by-moment basis. If someone's words weren't quite strung together the way I would string them, it could send me into a good cry. It was nice to have girlfriends like Gen who would just sit with an open ear to listen to all I was going through and all Jesus was teaching me. What a gift.

On that particular evening, I felt convicted to share my new ministry idea with Gen. The perfectionist in me wanted to present a perfect plan, fully fleshed out and foolproof. But to be honest, nothing about my new idea felt put together.

Any fellow perfectionists out there? Can you relate?

In that moment, my mind drifted to Galatians 1:10: "Am I now seeking the approval of man, or of God? Or am I trying to please man? If I were still trying to please man, I would not be a servant of Christ."

Then God spoke to me, saying, "This is not about you, Rebecca. It's about Me. This is not about your performance, your success, or your failure. It's about what Jesus did on the cross for you. It's not about your struggle. It's about wanting other souls facing tough life *stuff* to experience Me on a deeper level. This is a Me thing, not a Rebecca thing."

As usual, He'd spoken the words I needed to overcome my own insecurities and lean on Him. As I started to share my ideas with Gen, my plan wasn't pretty or put together. And it sure wasn't well-thought-out. However, I did it. I told my friend about this thing God was speaking into my heart. "I just can't shake it," I said. "I still don't know if God's really wanting me to step out in faith and actually start this thing or if I'm supposed to partner with something that already exists. I've searched and searched, and nothing feels personal enough."

As I shared how God had put Romans 8:18 on my heart, I knew somehow, in some way, I was supposed to incorporate that message into my ministry project: "I consider that the sufferings of this present time are not worth comparing with the glory that is to be revealed to us."

I explained that Mom had been encouraged by two things as she was going through chemo: handwritten notes from loved ones and the hats I crocheted for her. My desire was to combine those two comforts into a ministry that would serve others who were fighting similar cancer battles. My vision was to take groups into hospital settings to hand deliver hats and notes to patients.

While I excitedly shared my ideas, I realized I was seeking my friend's approval. Instead of relying solely on the prompting of the Holy Spirit to lead me, I felt I needed Gen's yes.

Until we become adults, most of our big decisions don't go unchecked by our parents, mentors, and friends. This is a good thing when we're young, but I needed to shift to adult mode when it came to stepping out in faith, especially because I was about to create something that didn't yet exist. The unknown landscape felt dangerously terrifying, and I longed for Gen's encouragement to fuel me forward.

But at some point in our lives, we stop needing permission slips to take steps of faithful obedience. No one was going to give me a stamp of approval that would echo louder than the voice of the Holy Spirit telling me I just needed to take the next step. Yet, in my own flesh, I had a laundry list of people whose input mattered to me. I longed to gain their approval before this new "thing" came into existence.

I would rather be pleasing in the eyes of God than be a success by the world's standards and miss the mark when it comes to all God has in store for my life.

When God tells us to do a new thing, sometimes we're nervous or fearful to begin. It's like staring at a blank canvas. We often feel we have to get everything right, as if it's all or nothing. We would do well to free ourselves of this pressure. When the Lord God of the universe has put on our hearts to serve Him in a new way, how often do we stall our own spiritual journeys by worrying too much about what people are going to think about us?

Wanna know the truth? It doesn't matter what other people think. It doesn't matter what they say. All that will matter in heaven is this: When the King of the Universe put it on your heart, were you obedient? I would rather be pleasing in the eyes of God than be a success by the world's standards and miss the mark when it comes to all God has in store for my life.

There is freedom found in running with abandon toward what is stirring in your heart. Hear me when I say that your glory goal won't make sense to everyone. However, it has been given to you by a pretty special Someone. Lean into the truths in His Word.

Deferred Obedience

We can have the best intentions when we start our project. We can pray about it and mull it over and line up all the steps to help ensure success. But sometimes we stall when it comes time to pull the trigger. Perhaps we fear there's someone out there who's more qualified, who has a better idea, or who has more confidence than we do. So we sit. And we worry. And we let all our insecurities take center stage.

Sound familiar?

I've learned that there are many flavors of **deferred obedience**, but they all stem from a similar root. *We're scared.* We don't know if our plans will work out, and we fear the unknowns. What if the finished product is not what we expected? What if people think I'm crazy? What if I waste time, money, or resources along the way?

Here's the problem. We will never run out of excuses, and we can never know the outcome as we make that first stroke across a blank canvas, but who are we to question God's invitation to us? Obedience deferred is disobedience.

Deferred obedience can look different for different personalities, and bringing our tendencies into the light is the first step toward pursuing our glory goal. By examining the many ways deferred obedience plays out, we can recognize roadblocks along the way and, more importantly, learn how to overcome them.

Start Too Big

First, you may be a **Start Too Big** kind of person. In this case, when you get a new idea, nothing in this world can stop you from seeing it through. Your fervor runs a few paces ahead of your logic, and you dive headfirst into everything!

If this is your default position, my mom and I raise our hands to salute you. As Start Too Big kind of gals, we both do the same. One of us will have an idea about a craft or hobby we want to start, and suddenly we're walking into the house, arms brimming with bags of resin, fake flowers, embroidery thread, polymer clay, and heaven knows what else. Sometimes the idea of starting something is a lot easier than actually doing it. We both have the spray paint stains and sore fingers to prove it. (Amen?)

In these situations, the feeling of being overwhelmed easily washes over us. That's why it's important to map out a plan with specific ways to move forward. (We'll spend a whole chapter on this later.)

Don't Know How

Others of us, when we consider this new endeavor we're doing with God, settle into a **Don't Know How** mentality. In this situation, we doubt we have the skill set to do the task, and we'd rather avoid it than fail. Doing something new for the first time is scary! We can't know the outcome or predict people's reactions as we create, but we'll never cross the finish line if we are not willing to even toe the start line.

To overcome a Don't Know How mentality, spend some time talking to God about your fears. He already knows them and, in fact, is already ahead of them. In these moments, you need a dose of Holy Spirit–induced courage. Ask God to give you wisdom and discernment in how to move forward, and be willing to say "YES!" when He makes it clear what your first step will be.

Excuse Giver

A third mentality that many of us can easily slip into is that of an **Excuse Giver**. In this case, we want to do the thing, but when we take inventory of our lives, we just don't see the bandwidth. Is a healthy view of our schedules a good thing? Absolutely! Am I condoning saying yes to everything? Absolutely not. As you will soon discover, I openly disagree with hustle culture. However, I have witnessed many friends sheepishly making excuses as to why they don't have the time or energy to answer God's call in their lives.

Are you willing to say an obedient yes to however, whenever, and wherever God calls? Don't let your current priorities stand in the way of what God has put in your heart. He may want to realign your situation. Joy and peace come on the other side of "Yes!" In a life that's sold out to God's leading, His glory is the goal, and His presence is the prize. This kind of yes may require sacrifice on your part, but trust Him!

> # In a life that's sold out to God's leading, His glory is the goal, and His presence is the prize.

Livin' on a Prayer Gal

Last, there's the **Livin' on a Prayer Gal**. In this case, we know God is inviting us into something new, but we haven't taken action. When friends ask about it, we say, "Yeah, I'm still praying about it!" as if to justify our inaction. I bet we've all been there.

We are commanded to continually be in an attitude of prayer (see Col. 4:2), and we should bring our requests to God always (see Phil. 4:6–7). He desires to talk to us (so please never stop going to Him). The trouble comes when we use prayer as an excuse for our stalling.

One of the greatest lies the Enemy plants in our hearts is that we need to keep on praying about the very logical, abundantly clear step God has asked us to take. If you're there, grab a friend today and talk about what your first logical step of obedience will be. I bet you already know what it is. What you need is the accountability of someone who will encourage you as you dare to live with great courage.

I am praying as I write that, no matter which personality you identify with, you will move with unabashed courage in the direction God is leading you.

Build the Plane as You Fly

The year my mom was undergoing treatments for breast cancer, I was in the middle of navigating this calling God had put on my heart to serve cancer patients. As I was praying through what the ministry would do and how we would best serve people, my grandparents were sharing my ideas with their pastor. He offered to partner with me and help me throw a launch event where people could come celebrate what God was doing and get involved.

I went to lunch with the pastor and his wife, and they both smiled as they listened to me describe all the not-so-perfectly put together thoughts I had about what God had placed in my heart. I rambled for forty-five minutes as they patiently listened, nodded, and asked questions along the way.

At some point, the pastor looked at me and said, "Rebecca, you don't have to have it all figured out. Don't be afraid to build the plane as you fly."

Sometimes we think that knowing all the answers will make our fears vanish. But common sense tells us this is not the case. God imparts His wisdom for each season He's placed us in. If we knew beyond that, our journey wouldn't require faith. We see evidence of this in Psalm 119:105: "Your word is a lamp to my feet and a light to my path."

Our God created not only the earth, moon, and stars, but He also created our brains, right? So let's use them wisely. Plan. Pray. Seek. And then don't be afraid to take steps forward as He guides and directs you.

Get the Wiggles Out

Morgan Harper Nichols is one of my favorite online creators. She paints digital art and shares the most beautiful words that some of us have ever seen stretched across Instagram. I've had the honor of hosting her on my podcast many times to chat about her work, her books, and the challenges creatives face as we pursue our callings.

The first time we talked, I told her about this very book (which I was working on at the time). When I shared about the idea of starting well, she said something I've not forgotten since:

"Sometimes you just have to get the wiggles out."

Sometimes, the first draft is not pretty. It's not complete or ready for the world's consumption. But it's the start that matters; we have to pick up the pen or the paintbrush or the microphone if we want to eventually launch that business, ministry, or whatever God is inviting us into.

When I rebranded my podcast in the summer of 2021, I created no less than seventy-five versions of the new cover art. I wanted to get it just right and spent months creating a brand kit that included fonts and colors and the overall personality we were aiming for as we developed this new identity for the show. But to be honest, the first design I created was the most difficult.

When I opened my laptop and began designing, I quickly realized the cover art needed to be reiterated many times before it truly would feel like "the one." Each day I would open it, make some tweaks, download a few options, and send them to friends for feedback. However, if I hadn't gotten the wiggles out on those first designs, I might still be stalling.

We have to get the wiggles out, build the plane as we fly, and trust that our blank canvas will become something beautiful in the end. By putting our faith fully in God, we can create with confidence.

Prepare for the Flood

A Bible story that never ceases to amaze me is the story of Noah. Even if you didn't grow up in church, you probably know this story. As Genesis 6 tells us, a ton of wicked sin was running rampant on the earth and it grieved God's heart. Noah, who had found favor in God's eyes, became the conduit through which our Creator preserved life.

What we tend to forget is that God gave Noah very specific instructions regarding a flood *that had not yet happened.* When we consider that Noah didn't have our modern conveniences, like being able to access information about the weather at the touch of a button, we realize just how faith-filled he must have been to obey God's call.

Although Scripture doesn't tell us what was going on in Noah's mind when God gave His instruction, it does tell us what Noah did in response (v. 22):

Noah did this; he did all that God commanded him.

This statement challenges me in my own starting of something new. In the newness, in the uncertainty, Noah did not cower in fear or delay in obeying. Instead, he said yes to God. And by doing so, Noah took God up on His invitation to become a part of a bigger plan for the world.

Sis, we have the same opportunity in our lives when God invites us to serve Him in a new way. We will not have all the answers. The project might seem a little crazy, especially to onlookers, and we may not understand why we're being led in that direction. But as James 1:5 tells us, "If any of you lacks wisdom, let him ask God, who gives generously to all without reproach, and it will be given him."

You see? We will not be left in the dark forever. Eventually, it will all make sense.

What if you put your name in that same sentence from Noah's story?

_____ did this; she did all that God commanded her.

What step might you need to take for this to be true for you? Again, you don't have to have the first ten steps figured out already. Just the first one. One step in the direction God is calling you. One yes to His master plan for your life. He will be faithful to reveal the next step and the next one as it comes.

Prayer Prompts

Use these prayer prompts to help you pray and journal about what God is revealing to you in this chapter.

God, will You help me:

- see areas of deferred obedience clearly in my life

- approach my blank canvas with the confidence that You've given me all I need

- remember You are the giver of creativity and joy

FOR THE GO-GETTER GIRL

SCRIPTURE FOR REFLECTION

- Galatians 1:10
- 1 Thessalonians 5:16–18
- Psalm 119:105
- James 1:5
- Genesis 6

GOALS

- God is awaiting your yes to His invitation. Is there an area of your life where you have deferred obedience?

GUMPTION

- What's an example of a place in your life where you are currently staring at a blank canvas? What fear or concern do you have around that?

GRACE

- Who are the key people you can turn to for wisdom and prayer as you take your next steps? Can you set a coffee date with them this week?

DO THE THING MANIFESTO

Review our manifesto statement for chapters 1 and 2. Depending on your learning style, you may want to write it down, share it with a friend, or say the words aloud.

I am a go-getter girl for the kingdom of God. I seek to make Jesus Christ known through my work and to live in dependence on Him as I use my gifts and talents.

By the power of the Holy Spirit, I take step after step toward the God-dream He has put in my heart. When I stare at a blank canvas, I'm certain He will give me everything I need to advance the gospel.

VIDEO 1 NOTES (CHAPTERS 1–2)

See the QR code on page 21 for the video link.

Chapter 3

SPIRIT-LED STICK-TO-ITIVENESS

As any runner can tell you, no one starts off running by signing up for a marathon. First I learned to run a mile, and then I worked up to a 5K, and then I tackled numerous half-marathons and a lot of intense training before building up the endurance to run 26.2 miles.

One day, during a training session, my lungs fatigued as the distance passed beneath my feet. With each harsh foot strike, my mental stamina was challenged beyond anything I had previously experienced. Since I'd never run a full marathon, my body didn't recognize this level of strain. I was bone-tired but still had 5 miles to go. Although I had crossed the finish line of many half-marathons and done other endurance activities, I was unsure if I could finish that first 20-mile training run.

I'd been warned this might happen, so I'd asked my running coach, Robin, to meet me at mile 18. Without her, I knew there was a chance I might stop early.

As I reached our meeting point, I could see she was checking her laces. Soon, off we went. Together. With her pacing beside me, she lifted my spirits and gave life to my tired muscles in a way I desperately needed, as if I had borrowed strength from her fresh legs. But the boost was short-lived. When we turned for the final stretch, I could go no farther. I stopped, put my head between my knees, took deep, long breaths, and started tearing up. "I can't do this," I whispered, shame and frustration blocking my voice.

Robin knelt, looked me in the eyes, and said, "Rebecca, you've made it this far. Think about it as if you're starting a 1-mile run. Don't think of the 19 miles you've already done. Let's go!"

With her cheering me through each passing second, one step at a time, we drew closer and closer to our cars. When I finally felt the vibration of my watch signaling I had finished the final mile, I cried right there in the parking lot.

When training for a full marathon, everyone at some point will feel like they're at the end of themselves. Oftentimes, as we pursue our glory goal, similar moments happen, when we have to develop some **spiritual stick-to-itiveness** to endure the final stretch.

Enduring to the end of an endeavor has been a through line in my life. There isn't a sprinter bone in my body. The slow churn is where I tend to thrive. Maybe that's why God leads me to long-run opportunities, the kind of situations where, rather than a short burst of ministry, there's a long season of just plain ol' not quitting.

In life, we must fix our eyes on Jesus in the same way I relied on Robin to strengthen me that day in training. This very book you hold in your hands is evidence of my long game. Seven years of my life went into pursuing the opportunity to become a traditionally published author. (Yes, I said seven years!) Some might ask, "How did you know not to give up?" The truth is, I didn't. The real truth is, many of us quit too soon.

Maybe you've been discipling the same group of women for a while and you don't seem to be seeing any spiritual progress. Perhaps you started a business that you're passionate about but it isn't growing quite as quickly as you anticipated. Maybe you've been recruiting volunteers for a community project and you haven't yet found the right support team. There are many challenges in life that can leave us feeling discouraged, as if we can't make it one step further.

This is when our not-giving-up, slow-churn attitude is crucial. I sum up this concept as *stick-to-itiveness*. It means "dogged perseverance."[1]

We can develop a Christlike tenacity when we walk stride for stride in submission to the Holy Spirit's leading and prompting.

I'll confess ... some days—most days—I don't feel very "dogged" about anything. But remember how in chapter 1 we learned that we do not operate by our own strength and that it's not all up to us to complete this journey? That same belief can help us walk forward with a confidence that God will lead us, even in those moments when *sticking it out* feels Oh. So. Hard.

We can develop a Christlike tenacity when we walk stride for stride in submission to the Holy Spirit's leading and prompting. We still do the work; we just know who is empowering us through every step. Of course, the Enemy will throw many obstacles in our way, hoping to make us cower with our heads between our knees, certain we can't handle what a life of faithfulness requires. So let's take a closer look at what these blocks might look like, and then let's learn how to overcome them and keep moving forward toward our glory goal.

Idea Blocks

The road to publishing a book is a long one, and the process has proven to be much more like a marathon than I ever imagined. Who knew writing a book would be such a long game? One of the first of countless steps is to submit a proposal with hopes a literary agent (and then a publishing house) will dare to get behind your idea.

The first time I sat down to work on my book proposal for this project many years ago, I was beyond excited. I felt God's direction concerning the core message He wanted me to work on: to help women see their gifts and talents from a gospel-centered perspective. However, I'd reached a point in the brainstorming where the ideas had stopped flowing. I had taken the step of obedience, bought the sticky notes, poured a cup of coffee, and then … somewhere along the way, the work started to feel hard. Too hard. My fingers no longer had words pouring out of them like they had in the beginning. *I was facing an idea block.*

An **idea block** happens when something or someone stands in the way of your glory goal. You know what you're aiming for and you know you're being led by the Spirit to go there, but you can't seem to shake this feeling of being stuck.

Regardless of who we are and what goal we're aiming for, several common blocks can stop our progress.

First, **we may be just plain weary**. We can easily believe that if we work a little harder, get up a little earlier, or keep going a little longer, then we can get there—wherever "there" might happen to be. But in truth, we don't need to work harder. In most cases, we just need to stop and catch our breath (or take a nap!). It's impossible to refuel your tank if you never put your mind in park.

My husband, Dustin, recently went on a fly-fishing trip out West and didn't have cell service for five days. At first, it felt strange to know we wouldn't have any contact for that long. But the closer we came to his departure, the more excited I became for him. Five days of rest away from the office, away from people, and away from social media? I couldn't think of anything better for his mental health as a pastor and husband, and I knew it would be pivotal for our church ministry (and it sure was). He came back refueled, having spent a quality week communing with God, and returned with a fresh outlook.

Now, I know what you're thinking. *Rebecca, I can't just pack up and fly to Wyoming to fly-fish with God all week.* I get it. I think too often we have extreme ideas of what refueling looks like. As a result, the entire concept becomes a mystical, unachievable fantasy. Sure, a week-long vacation isn't always possible, but a catnap usually is. Finding time to sabbath each week from our pace of life is a biblical command that God even modeled for us in the seven days of creation. We see in Genesis 2:3, "God blessed the seventh day and made it holy." *Why?* "Because on it God rested from all his work that he had done in creation."

Next, idea blocks can come when **we just plain don't know how to do the thing.** We may feel like we have it all figured out, but the unfortunate truth is that we are not omniscient. Only God can see the big picture. We must rely on the Holy Spirit to direct us through His guidance and through the people He sends into our lives.

It's no small thing to admit we need help. And to accept that help when it's offered. I wonder how many glory goals have been scrapped this year simply because someone was unwilling to ask for help. There are likely businesses that haven't been launched because of anxiety about the unknown, ministries that have delayed moving forward for fear of failure, and everyday nudges from God to offer an encouraging word or a kind deed that have been neglected because doing so might seem awkward or even costly.

Let's be the women who raise our hands proudly and ask, "Would you be willing to help me here?" or "I'm not quite sure where to take this. Can you point me in the right direction?"

Another very real culprit of idea blocks is **plain ol' rejection**. Talk about a stealer of joy and momentum! That said, rejection can also be one of our greatest teachers *if* we have the humility to be coachable.

Most times, rejection is a redirection toward what God is prompting us to do. But we must choose to see it through a lens of grace, accepting that a closed door is a hallway leading us toward the right door. In other words, rejection puts us one step closer to the thing that is *our* thing.

No matter what you bring to the pages of this chapter, God has put big glory goals inside you to make Him known. There's a good chance you feel a little shaky about taking that step of obedience. Maybe you're tired and weary and the idea of stick-to-itiveness feels exhausting to you. You may need to take some time away to renew your mind. You may need to bring in a fresh set of eyes to help you sort through the next steps. You may need to pivot in a new direction. Whatever it takes, don't shrink back just because you can't see the outcome yet. Promise?

A Season for Everything

Soon after my wedding, I knew in my knower that God was leading me to start a podcast. I had consistently managed a blog for a couple of years, proving to myself that I could produce content on a regular basis. But I was a tad leery about podcasting. *Did I have the personality? Who would listen? Would anyone want to be my guest?* Despite countless doubts, I knew God was leading me toward creating a show. With a new season of life, I had the time and resources to invest in launching it. And it felt logical to host it under the same name as my blog, which I eventually rebranded to *Radical Radiance*.

As I swiveled in my office chair and nervously tapped my pen on the corner of my desk, I said yes to God. I did some research, found a hosting tool, bought a cheap mic from Amazon, and wrote a list of dream guests to interview.

My husband, Dustin, would agree with me in saying that I have a scrappy personality. I'm always on the search for efficiency and, despite my desire to have everything figured out before I share an idea with others, once I'm comfortable with where I'm headed, I tend to live by the notion that "done" is better than "perfect." This attitude has served me well in my career thus far—a successful nonprofit that started in my college apartment, a blog turned podcast that was designed after watching endless DIY YouTube videos. As Alli Worthington says, "With God and Google, we can do anything!"[2]

Scrappy gets us past the start line. Intentional helps us endure the hard days.

It's tempting to wait until we have it all figured out. But we can't get hung up on having a Cadillac when a Honda will take us where we need to go. What do I mean? Nobody needs a microphone that costs hundreds of dollars when they launch their podcast. Does quality matter? Sure. We want to pursue our glory goals with excellence, always. But where there's a will, there's a way. Compromise, with a good measure of wisdom for what you truly need, is key.

Maybe you would like to start a business but some equipment you feel you need is currently out of your price range. Many times, we need to start small, and even run small for a while, until we get our feet underneath us. This can be a critical part of stick-to-itiveness. For many of us, it's very easy to delay a step of obedience because we don't have it all figured out or don't have the best of the best. We know we need to take the next step, but we let perfection be our barrier when we need to just get going!

That being said, there comes a point in our pursuit when it is worth the investment to upgrade. Scrappy gets us past the start line. Intentional helps us endure the hard days.

I was very successful in launching my show with a thirty-dollar USB mic from Amazon. I only upgraded my equipment once I knew I was in this podcasting thing for the long haul and had learned enough to know exactly what I needed to buy. By the time I made that big purchase, it was well worth the investment.

In your own life, there will be moments when God will lead you to make the intentional move over the scrappy one. Listen for His voice and be obedient to His leading.

Cute Little Side Hobby

A few weeks ago, I interviewed one of my very favorite authors for my podcast. We had an amazing conversation. After it was over, she was so kind as to say, "Good job, Rebecca. That was a great interview."

Now, what you don't know is that this author is known for her spitfire personality and bold proclamation of the gospel. She means what she says and says what she means, so her compliment meant *a lot* to me. As I sat and downloaded the audio file to begin editing, the Holy Spirit spoke to me: "This is no longer a cute little side hobby. Please stop treating it that way."

As I spent time in prayer, I repented for making light of the assignment God had given me. The truth is, I'm grateful He led me to create a podcast. I care deeply about using the show as a method of discipleship that can span the world with the click of a button. However, it's easy to see my ministry work as just a cute little side project, especially because I'm still working a traditional nine-to-five job (cue Dolly Parton).

Living in a small town in the Deep South and being a pastor's wife, it's easy to feel misunderstood. The women around me are primarily schoolteachers, mommas, and nurses. These are three of the *highest* and *holiest* callings for a woman. I truly believe that! However, I am none of those things. While I'm extremely grateful for the friendships that have developed in this season, it's very easy for our conversations to drift to snotty noses, soccer practices, and what we are going to do with a pack of chicken tenders tonight for dinner.

Our glory goals are never a cute little side hobby in the eyes of God.

At times when I'm asked about my work, which is incredibly kind, a chasm seems to open up between us. Often, they don't really know what to ask, but as friends, they show interest in my role as a writer and speaker. I love and appreciate those friends, but now and then I get the sense that my work may look like a cute little side hobby to other people. I wonder if you can relate. You begin sharing what you're working on, and you get that blank look that feels like one of the following statements glaring back at you:

> *She has very big dreams!*
> *I don't really get it.*
> *This all feels very foreign to me, and I'm not sure I want to understand.*
> *How cute!*
> *She is so driven, and I bet she will write that little book of hers one day!*

We've probably all walked away from at least one conversation feeling a tad discouraged, even if the person we were talking to had wonderful intentions. Maybe our insecurities took the wheel, or maybe the heart of the conversation felt shallow. But we shouldn't let other people's comments deter us from our work, especially if they don't understand our passions.

When someone makes our work seem insignificant (whether intentionally or not), we have a choice: listen to our insecurities or lean into God's voice as He continues to guide us. Our glory goals are never a cute little side hobby in the eyes of God. Let's refuse to allow other people's words to speak discouragement over the specific ways He has gifted us to bring Him glory.

You Are Doing a Great Work

God didn't leave us to face discouragement and distractions alone. Tucked away in the history books of the Old Testament is the story of Nehemiah, cupbearer to King Artaxerxes. Nehemiah may not be the most familiar book in the Bible, but we can learn a lot from the way he handled distraction from his enemies.

Nehemiah worked with an unwavering tenacity. What mattered to God mattered to him. In his day, a lot was happening in Jerusalem that was not advancing the kingdom of God. In fact, the region was an absolute mess. The wall bordering the city of Jerusalem had been broken down, and its gates had been burned. Total devastation.

As a result of this loss, Nehemiah wept and mourned. He cried out to God, admitting the Israelites had been disobedient to His commands.

In response, Artaxerxes sent Nehemiah to rebuild the wall. But two men, Sanballat and Tobiah, did everything they could think of, including taunting and ridiculing Nehemiah, to distract him from his sacred work.

The ultimate distractions came when Sanballat, Tobiah, and Geshem sent word saying they wanted to meet with Nehemiah on the plain of Ono. They wanted no part of the wall being rebuilt and were determined to prevent Jerusalem from thriving again. Five times they sent word to distract Nehemiah from the work God had called him to do, and five times he was faithful and refused to quit: "I am doing a great work and I cannot come down. Why should the work stop while I leave it and come down to you?" (Neh. 6:3).

Nehemiah had a choice to make. He could give in to peer pressure, come down off the wall, and be distracted by his enemies' cunning advances. Or he could keep showing up to do the thing he'd been called to do, even when he was weary, even when others seemed determined to stand in his way, even when the whole world seemed too far gone to help.

By remaining focused on the job at hand and faithful to God's plan, Nehemiah finished the project in fifty-two days.

So what does this ancient story mean for us today? Well, much like Nehemiah, we will all encounter discouragement as we set out to pursue our glory goal. Distractions and conversations might leave us feeling "less than" and misunderstood. We must remain steadfast in the face of these obstacles, which we can do only by the power of the Holy Spirit in us. We must walk step by step with Him, allowing Him to lead us, help us focus on what matters most, and enable us to get the help we need. We are working to make His name known to the ends of the earth (even if that means our little corner of it).

Prayer Prompts

Use these prayer prompts to help you pray and journal about what God is revealing to you in this chapter.

God, will You help me:

- develop a Spirit-led stick-to-itiveness in my work

- see rejection as a redirection from You

- see ways in which I can refuel and renew my mind

FOR THE GO-GETTER GIRL

SCRIPTURE FOR REFLECTION

- Ephesians 2:1–10
- Nehemiah 6
- 2 Corinthians 4:1–18

GOALS

- Read Nehemiah 6. What about Nehemiah's stick-to-itiveness encourages you today? Where might God be leading you to lean in and trust Him as you endure?

GUMPTION

- When have you experienced rejection? How can you turn that rejection into a life lesson to help propel you forward?

GRACE

- Where do you feel weary and need to refuel? What might Sabbath look like for you this week?

DO THE THING MANIFESTO

Review our manifesto statement for chapters 1–3. Depending on your learning style, you may want to write it down, share it with a friend, or say the words aloud.

I am a go-getter girl for the kingdom of God. I seek to make Jesus Christ known through my work and to live in dependence on Him as I use my gifts and talents.

By the power of the Holy Spirit, I take step after step toward the God-dream He has put in my heart. When I stare at a blank canvas, I'm certain He will give me everything I need to advance the gospel.

I persevere with a stick-to-itiveness that the Enemy cannot interrupt or thwart. I will not make light of what God has called me to do. He has called me to a great work, and I will not stop in the midst of discouragement or distraction.

Chapter 4

OWN THE ORDINARY

I have a confession to make (and be warned, I'm going to whine for a minute here, just to show you one of my weaker moments).

Like many people, I thought living out my book publishing dreams would be a little more glamorous than it's turned out to be. Picture this: I'm sitting crisscross applesauce in my home office with a mug of hot tea. It's Labor Day, and while I'd love to *not* labor on this holiday, I'm sitting here at 2:33 p.m. staring at this chapter head-on.

It would be a lot easier to put this task off until tomorrow. But for some reason it felt right to throw on some Chapstick, yoga pants, and a delightfully soft cardigan, grab a cup of ambition (another Dolly reference; you're welcome), and Do. The. Work.

Like many of you, I thrive on routines and meal plans, but I also scroll Instagram more than one should and can really excel at procrastination. Sometimes, even when I'm completely focused on the task at hand, my words don't seem to flow, and it takes me weeks to feel okay about a chapter (or a paragraph). I get stuck. Often. And I'm willing to bet you do too. But even when I experience those blocks, I'm encouraged that God never leaves me alone in the struggle. When I open my hands and surrender my every day to Him, His power is made perfect in my weakness (see 2 Cor. 12:9). God is the gap filler. He takes my meager offering and empowers me to do His good, acceptable, and perfect will, as Paul talks about in Romans 12:2.

In this chapter, we'll examine truths from God's Word and strategies to keep us moving forward toward our glory goal, even in moments when we'd rather be doing something else.

Third Lap of the Mile

My head pounded as I crossed the eight-hundred-meter mark and nodded at my running coach. Mile repeats. I loved to hate them as much as I hated to love them. They had become my kryptonite during this marathon training cycle. I would look at pictures of St. Jude patients on my phone during my recovery breaks to remind myself why I was running. Yet that didn't stop my lungs from working overtime as I entered the first curve of the third lap that day. Seemingly insurmountable fatigue settled into my quads, and my arms had to work twice as hard to maintain my pace. I almost stopped but … this mattered, I had learned. The not quitting in the middle of a 5:00 a.m. workout on a Tuesday was what resulted in things like my VO$_2$ max increasing and a host of other things that would make me a better runner on race day. The third lap didn't necessarily matter that Tuesday morning, but you'd better believe it would matter a lot come December when I hit the final stretch.

In the straightaway, another coach saw me struggling and began singing "Maybe It Was Memphis" as I gave him a strained look. I forced a half smile and replayed the faces of cancer patients in my mind. This was for them, to raise money to help them fight the war being waged in their bodies. This race represented something far weightier than a simple mile repeat. It was me locking arms with these children to fight cancer, just as others had locked arms with us years earlier when my mom was slaying her cancer dragon.

As I rounded into the fourth and final lap, my countenance lifted. One more training task was almost complete, which meant I was one step closer to the starting line of my race.

We experience many milestone moments in pursuit of our glory goals, so it's important to remember a few key tips to help us keep moving toward the finish line.

First, remember that **with each step forward, you're one step closer to the next step**. I use the metaphor of running throughout this book because just as running is about taking one step after another, most of our days are about taking one faithful step of obedience after another in a Godward direction. Some steps will feel hard; others more ordinary. But as disciples of Jesus Christ, we'll find that our lives look more like a long marathon than a sprint to the finish line (see Heb. 12:1–2). Just remember, our finish line—heaven—is holy and beautiful, and we should greatly look forward to it! But while we're here on this side of eternity, we must be faithful. We must press on. We must keep doing the work we are called to do.

Your obedient yes now will lead you toward what He has already prepared next for you.

Next, keep in mind that **you've already shown up**. Yes, I felt like quitting in the middle of that mile repeat exercise, but how self-defeating would that have been? I had already done the hard work of getting out of bed at 4:30 that morning and dragging myself to a predawn practice. My mental endurance needed to meet my physical endurance.

When our eternal perspective gets tested, we must remember that we are not walking through this assignment alone. God is with us, and He is for us. With deep faith, we can trust how the Holy Spirit is leading and guiding us, even when it doesn't always look like what we expect (like when the coach started serenading me to fuel me forward through the final laps).

Finally, don't forget—**this journey will be worth the risk**. God is at work within you as a unique expression of His glory in this world. Your obedient yes now will lead you toward what He has already prepared next for you. These steps are your training exercises. They are necessary and right and good, even if they feel difficult and monotonous and scary. Keep showing up. Every day. Because God's work in you is worth it. God's glory made known on this side of eternity is worth it. And on that final day, when He sets all things right in heaven, all your efforts will be worth it. Your hard work will be done, and you'll forever be singing His praises face to face.

Tomorrow

One of the most dangerous words we can use in our vocabulary is *tomorrow*. It's so easy to put off the hard thing because it's more gratifying to accomplish a smaller task.

For example, when I started 818 Ministries (the ministry I told Gen about in chapter 2), I always put "finish 501(c)(3) application" at the bottom of my to-do list. I knew it needed to be done if I was going to launch a nonprofit. I was just scared to jump in because of the time I knew it would cost me. I had never completed one of these applications, and the task seemed intimidating. For that reason, I took the easier road and kept procrastinating, coming up with excuse after excuse for each delay. Of course, this was just another block that was keeping me stuck in place. Eventually, I had to find a way to overcome it.

When doing God's work, we can't just stare at our planners and admire a well-thought-out to-do list. Sure, it feels good to check off the items that are easy, doesn't it? We thrive in the check marks until we reach a certain point in our day, and then, there it is. The gut check. The thing we need to show up for in our calling that sits there, unchecked. It's not that we don't want to do the thing. It's the going from here to there, if you will, that we struggle with.

Something happens in me when I tackle the thing I'm avoiding. I feel accomplished and confident, and the success serves as a great reminder that God will equip us for the job (even when that means getting some help). These celebratory times with God propel us forward and encourage our hearts as we continue His work.

Finishing the thing we've been putting off also enables us to receive what God wants to deliver next. I will never forget the day I packaged up all the paperwork for my nonprofit application and mailed it off to the IRS to launch 818 Ministries. It felt like such a special moment between God and me, a true test of my faith. Once that dreaded task was done, the brain fog that had accompanied this unfinished business was gone. I was ready to run fully in the direction of the next important season God had planned for the ministry.

Romans 8:28 tells us, "We know that for those who love God all things work together for good, for those who are called according to his purpose." I know you are called. I also know He is working all things, even this thing, together for His glory and your good. What unfinished business do you continue to put off until tomorrow? I encourage you to press into that hard thing, and then, when you're on the other side, you and God can celebrate together.

Insane Courage

As you pursue your glory goal, courage is key. When you feel overwhelmed, keep in mind that His yoke is easy and His burden is light (see Matt. 11:30). As a Christ follower, you don't need to move forward at a breakneck pace. You have the Holy Spirit living inside you to give wisdom. In your difficult moments, pause, take a deep breath, and remember He is with you. He is for you. He gives wisdom when you ask.

At a recent conference, I experienced one of these marked moments, and it challenged me greatly. I had joined fellow writers and podcasters for a late-night dinner where we each shared openly about what was working and what wasn't. When our server divvied out the plates of hot carbs and cheesy goodness, my friend Somer did something I'll never forget. She set her fork down and said, "Hey. We're about to pray over our food. Is there anything we could pray for you about?"

The server immediately teared up and shared about a family member who was ill and said that, while she was not a believer, she greatly appreciated our prayers. I prayed over her request, and when she walked away, our entire friend group was spurred on by Somer's step of insane courage. Was it scary for her to ask a stranger if we could pray for her? Maybe. But it encouraged me not to miss those opportunities in the ordinary moments in my own life.

Just as Benjamin Mee said to his son in *We Bought a Zoo*, "You know, sometimes all you need is twenty seconds of insane courage. Just, literally, twenty seconds of just embarrassing bravery. And I promise you, something great will come of it."[1]

I wonder what might happen if you showed twenty seconds of insane courage today. Chances are, as you read the story about Somer, you thought about something specific in your life that will require some bravery. Maybe you need to make a phone call about that volunteer opportunity you've been lying awake at night thinking about. Perhaps you feel led to mentor a younger woman, coach a team, deliver a meal … and maybe that next step feels scary. As Paul says, before he commands the church at Ephesus to put on the whole armor of God, "Finally, be strong in the Lord and in the strength of his might" (Eph. 6:10). You are strong because of the One who lives inside you. Before these moments that require insane courage, suit up, look up, and then (and only then) take that step forward.

Create Finish Lines

If there's something God and I wrestle about more than anything in my life, it's this idea of the long game. As mentioned, God has put me in very few places where my work has been a short sprint. But keep in mind, I didn't start off running marathons and writing books. First, I ran a lap and wrote a blog post. God leads me to things that require endurance, but I trust Him through the grueling journey it takes to get there. It's how I'm wired, I suppose.

As most creative people will tell you, it can be hard to keep the end in mind because the payoff feels so far away. We can say things like "Eat the elephant one bite at a time," but is that really helpful on a Tuesday when we feel overwhelmed? Probably not.

Sometimes, rather than a bigger goal, we need smaller steps. What if instead of getting bogged down in the big picture of it all, we celebrated each tiny step forward? To prevent burnout and overwhelm, create mini finish lines for yourself along the way. This is crucial when toiling through the exhausting stretches of ordinary.

Ordinary moments of faithfulness matter so much in the overall path of following Jesus.

When I took my first step as a runner, I didn't know for sure that it would eventually lead me to finish a full marathon. But I gave it my best shot, trusted God would strengthen me, and took my training one day at a time. We wouldn't be wise to drive from the Florida Keys to the Oregon coast without stopping along the way to savor the many beautiful places in between, right? Think about what's ahead of you, and break your journey up into small sections. Reward yourself by celebrating the wonders you experience along the way. This will help you see God's hand at work in every step.

For instance, if you're starting a business and the many tasks required to launch feel overwhelming, create small finish lines over the next six to eight weeks. This week, apply for your LLC. Next week, research any necessary business licenses you might need. The next, open your business banking account. Each task represents a small finish line on your way to completing the larger, big-picture glory goal that you're trying to accomplish.

These small feats are no small thing in the eyes of God. Ordinary moments of faithfulness matter so much in the overall path of following Jesus.

Who Am I?

Many of you may be familiar with the Bible story of a shepherd named Moses who cared for his father-in-law's sheep on the far side of the wilderness. At the time, this was considered a common but very important job. Tend to the sheep. Protect them. Herd them. Shear them. Repeat. It had to feel ordinary, don't you think? And perhaps it was … until it wasn't.

One day as Moses was leading the flock, he smelled smoke. When he found the source, he was shocked to see a bush that was on fire but not burning up. In this burning bush, God revealed Himself, telling Moses not to come any closer and to remove his sandals, for he was standing on holy ground (see Ex. 3:5). How peculiar for God to show Himself to Moses in this way. But in this way, God instructed this shepherd to go visit Pharaoh and lead the Israelites out of Egypt.

In this story, Moses asks, "Who am I?" (v. 11). He doesn't believe he is the right guy for this important job. God and Moses work it out, but the moral of the story is this: Most days of Moses's life did not involve God speaking to him through a burning bush. Most days were common ol' sheepherding kinds of days. They didn't seem spectacular in any way.

Our lives are much the same. Many of our days, pursuing our glory goals will seem, well, ordinary. That's not what we anticipate though, is it? We decide to give God our yes and then expect fireworks, or even a burning bush, when in reality God is just asking us to tend to the needs that are right in front of us.

Prayer Prompts

Use these prayer prompts to help you pray and journal about what God is revealing to you in this chapter.

God, will You help me:

- be aware of how You are at work in the mundane

- break up my goal into smaller steps

- see opportunities to love those around me (especially in everyday moments)

FOR THE GO-GETTER GIRL

SCRIPTURE FOR REFLECTION

- Romans 12
- Ephesians 6
- Matthew 11:25–30

GOALS

Sometimes we need to break large goals into smaller steps. Create a flowchart of mini finish lines that will help you move forward toward your glory goal. For example, to run a marathon, the following list of small finish lines would make sense:

START	START
Purchase a pair of tennis shoes.	
Research training plans.	
Find a training partner.	
Decide the day you will begin training.	
Follow the plan!	
FINISH	**FINISH**

GUMPTION

- In the middle of our "ordinary," we will have many "third lap of the mile" moments. What might it look like for you to move forward in faith this week?

GRACE

- God often finds us in our "ordinary" and speaks in unexpected ways, asking us to do things that seem impossible. Like Moses, we may doubt we're the right person for the job. Read Exodus 3 and reflect on which part of Moses's story you identify with most. Where is God leading you to extend twenty seconds of insane courage this week?

DO THE THING MANIFESTO

Review our manifesto statement for chapters 1–4. Depending on your learning style, you may want to write it down, share it with a friend, or say the words aloud.

I am a go-getter girl for the kingdom of God. I seek to make Jesus Christ known through my work and to live in dependence on Him as I use my gifts and talents.

By the power of the Holy Spirit, I take step after step toward the God-dream He has put in my heart. When I stare at a blank canvas, I'm certain He will give me everything I need to advance the gospel.

I persevere with a stick-to-itiveness that the Enemy cannot interrupt or thwart. I will not make light of what God has called me to do. He has called me to a great work, and I will not stop in the midst of discouragement or distraction.

Most days, my calling will look mundane. I will take small steps each day in a Godward direction.

VIDEO 2 NOTES (CHAPTERS 3–4)

See the QR code on page 21 for the video link.

Chapter 5

THE GENESIS OF STRIVING

I became acquainted with striving at a very young age, and before I knew it, it became my barometer of success. It's taken years to discern the difference between healthy achievement-driven behavior and toxic patterns that feed my ego. If I'm honest, I'm still a work in progress. (Aren't we all?)

When I look back on my history with striving, I can see myself in second grade. While my teacher handed out a quiz, I slumped down on my desk's armrest (which, having been made for right-handed people, served no other purpose for me as a lefty). While my pre-braces look left a lot to be desired, I had one thing going for me: multiplication tables. It was my mission to learn them like the back of my hand, and no one in that room was more prepared than me. With my pencil sharp and my determination strong, I tore through that quiz like my life depended on it.

When I indicated I had finished the test, my teacher lit up and danced across the room for my paper. She quickly graded it, announced I had a perfect score, and pointed out to the class that if they would practice like I did, they would be able to finish their quizzes with ease, just like me. This did a terrible number on my second-grade ego, and for the rest of the day I was on some sort of mathematics cloud nine, if there is such a thing.

You see, that's when it all started: $a + b = c$. If I work hard and hustle like mad, I will achieve "the thing," people will think highly of me, and I will receive the reward of praise.

Unfortunately, life isn't always quite as concrete as second-grade multiplication tables. One day, many years later, I found myself sitting in a high school calculus class. Mr. Peters, arguably one of the kindest and most effective teachers I've ever known, handed me a Scantron sheet (remember those?) to take my final exam. It was my senior year, and the stakes were high. At that moment I had a B in the class, but if I did well on the exam, I could potentially raise my overall grade to an A. Why did that matter so much? Well, up to that point, I had a maintained a 4.0 GPA. Perfectionist, much?

With baggy eyes and shaky hands from all the caffeine I'd consumed through days of studying, I took the test. I'll never forget walking up to his desk to wait for the results. While the other students were finishing, he quietly slid a torn piece of paper my way. Ninety-three, it said. I'd squeaked by, barely. (I still wish I could ask him if he rounded my grade up just so I wouldn't lose my 4.0. I guess I'll never know.)

When I entered adulthood, the stakes were much higher than the loss of a perfect GPA. I kept working hard, and, for a while, I achieved my goals even when it took blood, sweat, and tears. However, the more life I experienced, the more disappointment I faced. I was passed up for a promotion that would have been a big win for me. I trained for that marathon, running fifty to sixty miles a week, only to experience heat exhaustion on race day, crushing my goal of breaking four hours (as described earlier in the book). My friends, one by one, got married, and I continued walking down aisles in beautiful bridesmaid gowns instead of the white gown I longed to wear. I wondered when it would be my turn to get the promotion, break the record, and say, "I do."

At some point, we all have to face the reality that life often delivers circumstances that are completely out of our control. In fact, try as we might, striving usually leaves us burned out and resentful, longing for a life we wish we had rather than living fully into the life God has crafted specifically for us. Striving is an unkind friend, and after years of investing in that toxic relationship, I finally realized it was time to "break up."

I encourage you to do the same. For most of us, the roots of striving run deep and can be hard to sever. Stepping away from the never-ending striving doesn't mean we can't embrace ambition. We can and should throw ourselves fully into the gifts and talents God has graciously placed within us. But our efforts shouldn't be at the expense of our mental, physical, or spiritual well-being. Serving the idol of performance-based striving is exhausting. But God invites us into a different way of living, reminding us we are fully accepted and in right standing before God as followers of Jesus (see 2 Cor. 5:21).

Muscle Memory Takes Time

By now you know my husband, Dustin, is the pastor of a church in a small Mississippi town. To assimilate a little more into the culture, he agreed to go deer hunting with a friend and deacon named Bill. Now, the first thing you need to know about my husband is that if he commits to doing something, he's all the way in. There's not a lukewarm bone in his body, and he pours all he has into everything he does. It's one of the many things I admire about him.

When he decided to give deer hunting a try, he began shopping for bows. Most hunters, I quickly learned, use a compound bow for deer hunting. They are easier to draw and aim and, at times, can be much more powerful than the alternative: a recurve bow. A recurve bow is a stripped-down weapon with much more opportunity for error, but to Dustin, it felt like the most authentic tool to learn with if he was "really" going to become a hunter. So, after searching and searching, he found just the right bow for himself.

A few weeks later, the recurve arrived. Boy, was it a beautiful work of art, and he proudly found a space to display it in his "man room." In the days that followed, he prepped a spot out back where he could practice target shooting against an old shed. He would come home for lunch every single day, and even in Mississippi's midday humidity, outside he would go, bow in hand, ready to practice.

As his wife, I think there are few things more attractive to me than when Dustin sets his mind to learn something new. Lucky for me, my home office window looked out over our backyard to the very spot where he stood to practice. I admit, this was often the best part of my day.

Time and again, I watched him draw back and release that bow. At times, he nailed the bull's-eye and would look back at me in surprise while Jasper, our dog, would run a lap in celebration for him (as if he knew what had just happened). It became something we all looked forward to, and over time, the repetition produced great results. Dustin's aim improved, and he slowly felt more prepared for bow season.

He wasn't the only one who learned something from this new hobby. I gained a whole new perspective as I watched him practice day in and day out.

First, I watched him **focus**. Over time, he learned where to stand in relation to the shed, how to place his feet, and where to position his shoulders to get the most effective drawback. It took time, but once he learned, he became an efficient archer. Our work is much the same. Just as Dustin improved his aim by practicing multiple times a day, we, too, can become more effective with our time and talents so that doing our thing will become easier. Then, with systems and processes in place, we will become more effective in living out our calling.

Second, I watched Dustin be **faithful in repetition**. Repeatedly, he carried the bow outside and practiced. He didn't get frustrated with himself if he missed, nor did he expect to perfect his craft in the blink of an eye. He knew that the only way to move forward was by developing muscle memory and, man, did he build it. Many times, progress in our lives comes about the same way. It doesn't happen overnight by hustling like mad. It happens in the quiet, short pockets of time. These moments might seem insignificant at the time, but, in the end, they yield a great reward.

It's not about the extravagant deed but metered faithfulness.

Arguably the most important thing I observed was that **Dustin knew when to stop**. Most days, he would go outside and shoot for around fifteen to twenty minutes until he landed a good shot. Then, he'd raise his hands in victory to celebrate his arrow nearing the bull's-eye. And then he'd carry his gear back inside, done for the day. I would often think, *Don't you want to continue to build on that? What if you just stayed out a few more minutes? You could probably do it again!* Instead, Dustin savored each small improvement and let his brain remember what that last successful try felt like.

His approach challenged me so much. How often do we fail to stop and recognize our little improvements, hurrying on to the next thing or pushing ourselves past the point of exhaustion? What if we stopped, packed up our bows, and celebrated the one strike that offered proof we were doing good work just by continuing to show up day after day?

Many times we feel weary not because we're failing to make progress but because we desire to compress our progress into a shorter window than God has planned. Dustin's bow-hunting hobby taught me the power of sustained effort over a long period of time. It's not about the extravagant deed but metered faithfulness.

Cultivating an Unrushed Heart

I tend to run through life with all cylinders on go. It takes more work for me to slow down than it does to throw my hair into a messy bun and get something done. If the global COVID-19 pandemic taught me anything, it taught me to slow down my heart and my hands. For the first time in my life, my breakneck pace screeched to a halt and my days seemed to be happening in slow motion. Dustin and I would sit on the back porch in the evenings, listening to the wind and noticing each new burst of green in our backyard. I began savoring the new growth on our holly tree, and each time a new Egyptian star cluster burst open, I would rush out the sliding glass door to gawk over it.

Isn't it crazy how parts of our lives have been blossoming and growing, and all the while we've been too busy to notice? I often wonder what would happen if we oohed and aahed and delighted over how God is at work in our lives, much like the way I began to notice winter turning into spring during the pandemic. Would joy and contentment come easier if we stopped to notice the beautiful blooms being birthed in our daily lives?

One of the greatest practices I've found to help me see God's hand at work is to write letters to the Rebecca of a year ago. The girl I used to be has come a long way in just a year's time, and so have you. Forcing ourselves to think about what was happening 365 days ago forces us to reckon with what God has done, reminding us of how His glory is on constant display in our lives.

Peace is possible when hope is present. Jesus promises His peace to us in the Gospels: "These things I have spoken to you while I am still with you. But the Helper, the Holy Spirit, whom the Father will send in my name, he will teach you all things and bring to your remembrance all that I have said to you. Peace I leave with you; my peace I give to you. Not as the world gives do I give to you. Let not your hearts be troubled, neither let them be afraid" (John 14:25–27).

Did you catch that? We don't receive peace from anything the world offers us. Not from success, accolades, a promotion, an engagement ring, a book deal, or the next big step. Those are all great things and should be celebrated, but they are not the Source in which we anchor our ambition. No, that source is Jesus. His peace. His way. For His glory alone.

When we reach out and accept His invitation to this type of peace, the slowdown will begin to feel a lot more natural. Our striving will cease in the presence of our sovereign, all-knowing God.

Living in His peace is step one toward freedom, removing the anxiety and angst that come along with striving. When we're bound to the chains of striving, we tend to expect the same from those around us. Grace is impossible to extend until we first receive it for ourselves.

Of course, freed people free people. So as we learn to receive His peace, we will begin to see opportunities for us to free other "hostages" from their own striving too.

Doing versus Being

Our deepest places of struggle, when surrendered to God, can be the very places from which God moves in the most powerful ways. One day, as has happened many times during the writing of this book, Danielle and I were going back and forth about the topic of striving when she said something that really challenged me: "I think God is teaching me that the results are up to Him. The outcome and how His glory is best shown in a situation is not on me. I'm finding that the condition of my heart matters more than anything."

She couldn't have been more right.

The root of my striving has more to do with the condition of my heart than the length of my to-do list. I can work my tail off for the glory of God while also prioritizing abiding in Christ. Whether I'm presenting on a stage or sitting on the couch, my value in God's eyes remains the same. Our lives ebb and flow; there are times of work and times of renewal. As long as our hearts are surrendered to Him and we're being led by the Holy Spirit, we are headed in the right direction.

In John 15:1–5 Jesus tells us:

> I am the true vine, and my Father is the vinedresser. Every branch in me that does not bear fruit he takes away, and every branch that does bear fruit he prunes, that it may bear more fruit. Already you are clean because of the word that I have spoken to you. Abide in me, and I in you. As the branch cannot bear fruit by itself, unless it abides in the vine, neither can you, unless you abide in me. I am the vine; you are the branches. Whoever abides in me and I in him, he it is that bears much fruit, for apart from me you can do nothing.

Sometimes we want so badly to be the vine when He asks us to be the branch. Of course, the branch can't thrive apart from the vine. We are useless without our Life Source.

Every good, edifying thing we do comes when we are anchored to the Vine. The fruit doesn't come from our own efforts to claw our way to success "for the sake of the gospel." Striving and abiding can't cohabitate in the same heart. Letting these two forces compete for our affection is exhausting, isn't it? But the good news is this: we can lay down our medals and our pretenses. In Christ, the pressure is off!

Letting go of striving is going to be a daily choice for us as we move forward in our callings. To be faithful here, we need a plan.

First, **we must identify the root of our striving**, which may run deep in your life. Take some time to think about when you first got the idea that you had to hustle or strive for success or approval. Did you learn it while playing sports? At school? At church? Did an adult put pressure on you? Or was it an inner drive based on your personality and the cultural messages you received?

The root of my striving has more to do with the condition of my heart than the length of my to-do list.

It's important not to blame anyone or shame ourselves as we identify the origin of this root in our hearts. But we must name it so that it no longer has power in our lives. By recognizing where in our past this belief originated, we can declare it will have no part of our future.

As we begin to recognize patterns, it's important that we talk to God about our struggles. He was there when this pattern first took hold, and He is with us now as we work through this paradigm shift. He knows us so well and cares for us so deeply. He knows where our striving began, and He walks with us as we release our grasp on it. He's kind and extends unmerited grace when we repent for trying to take control from Him.

When Dustin and I visited the garden of Gethsemane on our tour of the Holy Land, our tour guide pointed out the olive trees that had been growing in the garden for at least two thousand years. Talk about strong roots! The more time that passes, the more the roots grow deeper and stronger.

The same can be said about us. If, like me, you're uprooting some roots that have been around since second-grade math class, you may be digging for a while. You may have to keep giving this over to God again and again as old habits kick in and you revert to hustling. Remember, this journey is a long game of endurance, not a sprint. Keep taking those steps of obedience, and God will lead you exactly where you need to be.

We Can Do Both

Abiding in Christ means leaning into the power of the Holy Spirit and leaning less on our own ability. It's working out of a holy ambition, but it's not straining to build our own kingdom.

The troubling thing is, we think we can't have both rest and work. We think we can't build a growing ministry while also practicing a Sabbath lifestyle. We think we can't be faithful to our calling if we're not working ourselves to the bone. Friend, those beliefs simply are not true. We are redeemed by an infinite God who has big plans for how He desires to use our gifts for His glory. And better yet, He did not leave us to figure all this out on our own.

Scripture tells us that hard work and self-discipline are crucial to a life of faithfulness as a Christ follower. Where we get it wrong is our belief that we're working for some type of approval or accolades from other people. We forget that the only true goal should be to honor God. Because He holds us in His favor and offers us unconditional grace, He will lead us toward assignments that make our hearts swell. He also sets forth a pattern for us to refuel, walk in community with other believers, and invest in discipleship. When we judge these things by worldly standards, we might feel they are not important enough. We are fools to think that His kingdom measures our acts in this way.

She Chose the Good Thing

Are you familiar with the Bible stories of the two sisters Martha and Mary? We're told about them twice: in the book of Luke and again in John. In the Luke story, as Jesus enters their village, Martha goes out of her way to welcome Him, tending to everything He might need. Meanwhile, Mary sits at His feet intently listening to His teaching. Frustrated that she's the only one working, Martha asks Jesus to tell her sister to come help her serve. She complains that Mary had left her alone with all the responsibilities.

Some readers give Martha a bad rap. She can't sit still, and she's preoccupied by all the wrong things, even when the Messiah, the Son of God, is present in her home. Some may even read this passage with a prideful heart, believing they would've been sitting right there with Mary at Jesus' feet hanging on to His every word. However, our lives often reflect a much different reality.

In Luke 10:41–42, we're told that Jesus responds to Martha with these words: "Martha, Martha, you are anxious and troubled about many things, but one thing is necessary. Mary has chosen the good portion, which will not be taken away from her."

What can we learn from Jesus' words?

Perhaps He wants to be in close relationship with us more than He wants us to be busily striving to please Him. Martha was busy, but was she fruitful? Mary was arguably the wisest with her time that day, and we too have the same opportunity to make choices that bring us close in fellowship with God.

If left to our own devices, we, like Martha, may gravitate toward activity, busying ourselves to exhaustion and doing it all in the name of God. But Scripture makes it clear that we must choose each day to stop striving and do the better thing—sit at His feet to know our Savior more intimately and to hear His truth in our lives.

Prayer Prompts

Use these prayer prompts to help you pray and journal about what God is revealing to you in this chapter.

God, will You help me:

• see where my roots of striving began so I can slowly dig them up and surrender them to You

• develop an unrushed heart that is focused on You

• see the fruit of what You've done in my life in the last year

FOR THE GO-GETTER GIRL

SCRIPTURE FOR REFLECTION

- Joshua 4
- John 14:25–27
- John 15:1–5

GOALS

- In what way is God prompting you to adopt Mary-like behaviors and sit at His feet to build intimacy with Christ?

GUMPTION

On the next page, take some time to write a letter to the you of 365 days ago. Recount the faithfulness of God that you have seen mark your life over the last year.

GRACE

- When did the tendency of striving begin for you? How does it impact your life today?

Dear _____,

With a thankful heart,

_____

DO THE THING MANIFESTO

Review our manifesto statement for chapters 1–5. Depending on your learning style, you may want to write it down, share it with a friend, or say the words aloud.

I am a go-getter girl for the kingdom of God. I seek to make Jesus Christ known through my work and to live in dependence on Him as I use my gifts and talents.

By the power of the Holy Spirit, I take step after step toward the God-dream He has put in my heart. When I stare at a blank canvas, I'm certain He will give me everything I need to advance the gospel.

I persevere with a stick-to-itiveness that the Enemy cannot interrupt or thwart. I will not make light of what God has called me to do. He has called me to a great work, and I will not stop in the midst of discouragement or distraction.

Most days, my calling will look mundane. I will take small steps each day in a Godward direction.

I will create with an unrushed heart, knowing I am operating out of an overflow of my private relationship with my Creator. Striving can cease when I operate by His agenda.

Chapter 6

THE INVITATION TO A FINISHED WORK

When I visit my family in Tennessee, we dedicate every moment to making up for the time we've spent apart. As a result, silence is rare when we're together. During one visit, Mom looked at me and said, "So … do you have an idea of what you might do with 818 Ministries?"

Mom must have known I'd been struggling. The thing is, as soon as Dustin and I had walked the aisle and said "I do," life as I knew it drastically changed. Not only did I shift from being a single woman to becoming a lead pastor's wife, but due to Dustin's position in Mississippi, I had moved nine hours away from Knoxville, leaving everything I had ever known. I was excited to enter this new season of great blessing, but it was difficult to loosen my grip on the wonderful life I'd left behind.

We can only wear so many hats before we eventually have to remove a few. Just as God prunes our branches so we can bear more fruit, I was being pushed to prune my life. As new relationships and responsibilities came to us, I knew something had to give. But every time I thought about giving up 818 Ministries, my heart grieved. How could I just walk away from the work God had called me to do? Having walked through my mom's cancer journey, this passion cut so close to my heart that I couldn't fathom moving on from it, especially after I'd poured so much time and energy into building it into a thriving outreach.

But my life was now full of podcast interviews, a new community of women to encourage, and, for goodness' sake, a husband to walk alongside as he shepherded the flock we'd been given in our church. Plus, I had finally been offered an opportunity to write this book.

Immediately, tears began to stream down my face as I said to Mom, "I really think it may be time to move on." Just saying the words brought me so much freedom, alleviating tremendous weight from my shoulders, but the encouragement that followed from Mom is a conversation I will never forget. "Rebecca," she said. "You were faithful to every ounce of what God had for that ministry. I know because I watched you. If it's time to move on, I think that's amazing, and while you don't need my permission to be faithful in your next steps, if you need me to affirm that for you, I will!"

It is quite possible that you, too, may be facing a season of transition in your life. When God compels our hearts to action, we often feel that it's a forever assignment when sometimes it's not. Seasons change, kids grow up, we relocate, and life itself can throw curveballs that change our plans. Even when our hearts are set on God as we create, we can feel a little lost when a season comes to an end. Let me be your voice of encouragement if you're struggling to let go as God prunes your life: trust His plans, and follow Him into this new direction.

Starting Strong versus Finishing Strong

We've spent a great deal of time in this book covering the process of starting well and enduring in our mission for Christ. We must also remember the importance of finishing strong.

As children, we all learned the principle of not giving up. Endurance was celebrated while quitting was looked down on. Listen, I get it. It's no new thing to claim that enduring to the end of an assignment God has given us is worthy and good and right. But we often fail to celebrate when God allows our plans to zig and zag.

There is always grace for the overworked but often not for the redirected.

What if you and I change this narrative? What if we celebrate our sister who feels called to a new season of ministry or a new assignment? More importantly for you, what if you let go of the shame of quitting an assignment that is complete? Stepping fully into this season of your glory goal will likely require that you let go of a few tasks or assignments that you hold dear right now. To move on, we must let go.

My husband has a great working definition for *hope*: **"a confident and favorable expectation of a future reality."** Isn't that how we should look toward new horizons? As we let go of something from our past that we hold close, we must rely on the Holy Spirit to give us an unrelenting hope as we press on.

If God has truly put this new thing on your heart, He is faithful and able to extend grace and gumption so that you may walk fully into what is to come.

Macroquitting versus Microquitting

We mostly think of quitting as involving big decisions or radical change. I call this level of transition **macroquitting**. The kind of life pivot that drastically changes the way we spend our days, macroquitting usually requires special skills, time, and/or resources.

You may be navigating this type of season now. But not all changes are big. Sometimes we may need to make simple pivots, called **microquitting**. Just as a ship that is one degree off course can end up at a different location, the course of our lives can change dramatically when we make small adjustments. In your life, this course correction might look like delegating a task, simplifying a process, or creating a plan to make space for the thing you feel God has placed on your heart.

Our lives will have times of both macroquitting and microquitting. It's important that we approach them both with intention and care. In this chapter, let's focus on seasons of change, big or small, and how we can effectively move forward in God's purposes for us.

Efficient Inefficiency

In my first job after college, our human resources team conducted an annual exercise called **Start-Stop-Continue**. I hated it (sorry, Jenny!). Anxiety always stirred in me as we examined our current processes to identify areas of inefficiency.

As a team, we would put giant Post-it notes on the walls and list areas where we felt we needed to start, stop, or continue a certain service we were offering our employees. Often, we would challenge one another if someone did not feel it was possible to stop a certain task (sometimes that someone was me!). I still think of those meetings all these years later as I work through areas of improvement in my own life.

Sometimes we become efficient at being inefficient. We know we need to move forward but, in the moment, it feels more difficult to stop or reinvent that "thing" than it does to continue in our comfortable pattern. As a result, we waste precious time that could be better invested in other tasks or projects.

Today, **start** by thinking about the small areas of your work: the processes, the workflows, the spaces where you're comfortable. Is there room for improvement? Whether it would require a substantial change (macroquitting) or a small tweak (microquitting), what would it look like to **stop** your current process and then **continue** moving forward in a more efficient way?

Here's Who You Need

As we become better quitters, we're going to need a few people in our corner. It's very important to choose your team wisely.

First, you need a **Been There**. Been Theres have already made this kind of move and walked through thought processes similar to the ones you are now facing. They know the efficiency that comes with a long-standing process, and they fully understand why you are comfortable, not wanting to step outside the box and make improvements.

Danielle is my Been There. I don't have enough fingers or toes to count the number of times she has walked me through decisions about how to make something better, faster, or more efficient. Because she had already experienced a season when God led her ministry in a different direction, her encouragement helped me let go when God called me away from 818 Ministries. With the wisdom of Been Theres, you do not have to reinvent the wheel. There's comfort in gleaning from their experience as you move forward.

The second person you want in your corner is a **Logical Improver**. While these friends may frustrate you at first, they'll be your most valuable asset. They do not approach decisions with emotion in mind. They think critically from a place that keeps your best interest front and center. They think long-term. They can see the forest, if you will. My husband, Dustin, is a Logical Improver. He's the person I go to first if I truly need an unbiased opinion from someone who loves me well but won't let my emotions be the main driver.

Last, but definitely not least, you need an **Encouraging Cheerleader**. When decisions are hard and fatigue sets in, you must have an enthusiastic advocate and confidante to celebrate your successes. These people offer a safe place to land when the going gets tough. My mom is my Encouraging Cheerleader, the one I call when I need a pick-me-up. Maybe that's why God used her to prepare me to move on to a new season.

If you are anything like me, you want your opinions to be affirmed by those you love. However, due to their wisdom and logic, Been Theres and Logical Improvers are just as important as Encouraging Cheerleaders in the process of microquitting and macroquitting. When you have these three allies in your corner, you can remain centered and ready for what's next: your glory goal!

A Multi-Passionate Mission

A trend of side hustling has emerged in the last several years. According to Zapier, one in three Americans currently have some sort of side hustle outside of their nine-to-five.[1] This number is expected to grow exponentially in the wake of the global pandemic, suggesting that, generationally, we are a people of passions. In fact, most of us have more than one!

I coach women in our community who often wrestle with the idea of being multi-passionate. As God calls us in and out of seasons, balancing our time and passions is a delicate dance and one worth discussing.

Praise God, we are not one-dimensional in our pursuits! God has likely gifted you with many talents that can be used for kingdom work, from the boardroom to the classroom to the local church and community. Rather than feeling overwhelmed or guilty that our lives are filled with different assignments, let's celebrate the many opportunities we are given. When we keep our priorities in their rightful places, there is absolutely nothing wrong with a good side hustle.

God may give you many hats to wear. This does not mean you have to wear them all at once. Saying no, delegating, and creating efficient processes are all very doable parts of maintaining a healthy, balanced lifestyle for you and your family. As seasons change, priorities follow suit, and we must rely on the Holy Spirit to give us wisdom and discernment about which passions should take third priority in our lives. I say "third priority" as I think back on a family principle Dustin and I established before we got married. With the constant demands for our time and attention, we knew it could be easy for us to get sucked into the demands of being "needed" at the expense of our family or even our personal relationship with Christ. (Yes, I said it.)

Here's the thing: we want our family, our church, and our faith to last. We want to endure. I think you do too. That is why, in our family, Jesus comes first. Our time spent in the Word and in prayer cannot be compromised or else our ministries will follow suit.

Next, we are each other's second priority. I have made sacrifices so I could better support my husband, and he has done the same for me. Our assignments in our respective creative ministries come third. Do we get it right all the time? No. Are there times when we sacrifice time with each other to go spread the gospel or take on something extra at church? Absolutely. But at the end of the day, we agree on our ultimate priorities, which then cascade down to our mission and help us determine how we spend our time.

Focus on doing *the* thing really well rather than doing *all the things* with mediocrity.

You and I have already established that we cannot do it all. But when we look around and see everyone seemingly "killing it" in their various pursuits, we can start to feel like we'll never keep up. The truth is, we won't. We can't. And that's because we were never designed to keep up with everyone else.

My best piece of advice to a multi-passionate creative is to *not* try to do it all at once. Instead, follow the age-old mantra: work smarter, not harder. Just focus on doing *the* thing really well rather than doing *all the things* with mediocrity.

Your Invitation to Celebrate

As you take inventory of your time, there is a good chance that a pivot or a shift may be necessary to carry you into what is next. As I debated quitting 818 Ministries, I had an important choice to make. I allowed myself to spend a little time grieving the loss of a season I loved. However, as time passed, I knew it was time to move on.

The brave choice was to praise God as I looked fully in the new direction He was taking me. In the Gospels we see that Jesus walked on water as He approached His disciples in a fishing boat. The men were terrified, and rightfully so. After Jesus had reassured Peter that it, indeed, was Him, Peter stepped out of the boat in faith, as Christ had commanded (even though the wind raged and the waters swayed).

> ## You will carry your past learnings and experiences into the next season.

Sometimes our steps are shaky, and the waves of doubt will rise. But in those moments, hear Jesus whisper, "Take heart; it is I. Do not be afraid" (Matt. 14:27).

Whether He's asking you to macroquit or microquit, take that first step out of your boat today. Walk toward Jesus faithfully, and He will extend the grace and ability to reach the outcome He has planned for you.

Just as my mom gave me permission to step away from 818 Ministries and walk fully into my new passions, I am extending an invitation to you now to let go and step into this new season. When you turn the page to begin a new chapter, do not fall for the lie that says that part of you is over. That part of you is still very much alive, and you will carry your past learnings and experiences into the next season. Let God develop a rich, unrelenting hope in you as you look toward the future.

Whatever Whenever

Sometimes God weaves major change into our story, and other times He calls us to faithfully plant our feet in a place or with a people. As I scan Scripture to find others who were unwavering in their obedience to God, I'm reminded of Ruth, whose faithfulness serves as a great model of making kingdom-minded decisions.

In the wake of losing her husband and two sons, Ruth's mother-in-law, Naomi, wanted to return to Judah because she'd heard the Lord had visited and provided food for His people there. She encouraged her two daughters-in-law, Ruth and Orpah, to go back home to their own families and prayed the Lord would deal kindly with them (at a time when widows were not treated very kindly at all). Orpah returned to her people as Naomi suggested, but Ruth stayed by Naomi's side, refusing to leave her alone: "Do not urge me to leave you or to return from following you. For where you go I will go, and where you lodge I will lodge. Your people shall be my people, and your God my God. Where you die I will die, and there will I be buried. May the LORD do so to me and more also if anything but death parts me from you" (Ruth 1:16–17).

If you know the story, you know that Ruth followed Naomi as she felt God was calling her to do, and in return, God provided for them both.

We must do the same. When God reveals that a season is coming to a close, we need to tighten up our shoelaces and prepare for where He is leading us next. He is sovereign and able to guide us as we listen to His voice.

Can you say the same yes that Ruth said to God's plan? Is your answer yes to wherever and whenever He leads?

Prayer Prompts

Use these prayer prompts to help you pray and journal about what God is revealing to you in this chapter.

God, will You help me:

- follow You wherever and whenever You lead

- discern when You are trying to communicate to me that an assignment is over

- be aware of and invest in the relationships I need to walk through seasons of quitting

FOR THE GO-GETTER GIRL

SCRIPTURE FOR REFLECTION

- Matthew 14:22–33
- the book of Ruth

GOALS

- Think about the ideas of macroquitting and microquitting. What tasks, projects, or assignments might God be leading you to stop at both levels?

GUMPTION

- Is there anything God might be prompting you to let go of to make room for something new? Are you saying yes to God's direction?

GRACE

- As you walk through these changes, which friend type do you feel you need the most in your life right now—Been There, Logical Improver, or Encouraging Cheerleader?

DO THE THING MANIFESTO

Review our manifesto statement for chapters 1–6. Depending on your learning style, you may want to write it down, share it with a friend, or say the words aloud.

I am a go-getter girl for the kingdom of God. I seek to make Jesus Christ known through my work and to live in dependence on Him as I use my gifts and talents.

By the power of the Holy Spirit, I take step after step toward the God-dream He has put in my heart. When I stare at a blank canvas, I'm certain He will give me everything I need to advance the gospel.

I persevere with a stick-to-itiveness that the Enemy cannot interrupt or thwart. I will not make light of what God has called me to do. He has called me to a great work, and I will not stop in the midst of discouragement or distraction.

Most days, my calling will look mundane. I will take small steps each day in a Godward direction.

I will create with an unrushed heart, knowing I am operating out of an overflow of my private relationship with my Creator. Striving can cease when I operate by His agenda.

I hold my plans loosely, relying on God for wisdom and discernment about which assignments should come and go in my life. I will prayerfully follow His lead, wherever and whenever He calls me to go.

VIDEO 3 NOTES (CHAPTERS 5-6)

See the QR code on page 21 for the video link.

Chapter 7

ILLUMINATE THE TALENT AROUND YOU

When acclaimed Bible teacher Lisa Harper joined the interview for my podcast, her earrings dingle-dangled and her camo jacket screamed, "I mean business about Jesus!" This was a dream interview for me, as I'd long admired her spunk and passion for advancing the gospel.

We had a great conversation and, to this day, it's still among my favorites. However, what happened after our official recording is what made my first encounter with Lisa unforgettable. She looked at me and said, "Rebecca, this is presumptuous, but I can go there because of my age. You are really, really called to teach. What you say carries weight. It's that Samuel thing where your words don't fall to the ground. So whatever I can do to help you, I want to."

Overwhelmed by her kind show of interest in my work, I blubbered out that my agent and I were working on my book proposal and would hopefully pitch it to acquisitions editors soon. Lisa went on to share about not settling and even dropped names of some folks she hoped my agent would pitch my idea to.

What she was not aware of was that I had fought for this idea for so long. God knew I desperately needed her encouragement, and He prompted her with the exact words that kept my weary heart going during the long and agonizing process of writing, pitching, and publishing a book. Her gift of unmerited grace encouraged my weary heart, stoking the embers that had grown cold with rejection and exhaustion.

Lisa didn't know that, years earlier, many a publishing house had said a kind "no" or "no for now" to my idea. But God knew I needed encouragement to keep me clinging to the hope that He had a plan for this book. And just when I was about to give up, God used Lisa as a go-getter gal who had the humility to stop and pour into the generation coming behind her. She became a conduit for God's encouragement to reach me and keep me going.

Why does this matter to you? Because you have been placed in a community, church, and/or friend group that I may never meet. You have been given the chance to impact their lives in meaningful ways, the way Lisa impacted mine. You were crafted by a creative God with the exacts gifts you need to fulfill this mission: "For as in one body we have many members, and the members do not all have the same function, so we, though many, are one body in Christ, and individually members one of another" (Rom. 12:4–5).

We are all part of the same body, but we all have different talents that carry the gospel forward. Begin to recognize these talents in those around you. Spur them on to do their thing too.

Like Lisa, you will have opportunities, orchestrated by the Holy Spirit, to pull along someone whose flame has been reduced to embers. And guess what happens when you stoke someone else's embers? It reignites your own fire.

Don't miss the Holy Spirit's invitation to illuminate the talent around you. To have zeal is to love what God loves and to delight in what brings Him joy. Sometimes, all someone needs to shine their light a little brighter is one person to call out their gifts. What if we all made that our mission?

Deep-Rooted Community

Part of illuminating the talent around us involves allowing other people to be a part of what God is doing in our lives. I experienced the power of this in the most profound way last year through my intern program.

A couple of years ago, I was drowning as the *Radical Radiance* podcast continued to grow. There were edits to be made. Freebies to be published to serve our growing audience. A website to be redone. I had mentally committed to doing a special Christmas series on the podcast. There was also the book proposal (that had yet to be polished and pitched to publishers).

I felt very sure, like, so sure, that God was calling me to this work of writing and speaking. On days when I felt overwhelmed, doors continued to open and I continued trusting God in the process. But I couldn't run at this pace much longer. I was also, like many of you, working a full-time job. Ministry was my side gig, one that was quickly turning into a full-time pipe dream.

One day, out of sheer desperation, I put up a call for volunteer interns on my Instagram stories. I couldn't hire help. Heck, I wasn't yet making money at this podcast thing! I prayed and asked that God would lead me to the right college girls in need of some experience who could walk with me through this season of growth. I held my breath and published the post. I came back later to a couple of applications from students who seemed like they could really contribute to the direction the ministry was going.

When I met with them on Zoom to learn more about their testimonies and goals, I fell in love with each of them for wildly different reasons. Nicole was confidently certain that she could figure most anything out with the help of Google and the marketing courses she had taken in college. She wanted to learn more about Pinterest and was a wicked organizer. I knew I could, for the most part, hand her anything and feel confident it would be completed with excellence.

Emilee was, and is, insanely passionate about carrying the gospel forward. She was fiercely creative and wise beyond her years. Like me, she loved helping other women and wanted to see them walk confidently and freely in who they were in Christ. That fire drove every project she worked on, including the development of an amazing lead magnet, weekly graphics for the podcast, and the materials for an online conference. All things that I wouldn't have been able to accomplish fully without her.

In Ecclesiastes 4:9–10, we see evidence that it's good to have help: "Two are better than one, because they have a good reward for their toil. For if they fall, one will lift up his fellow. But woe to him who is alone when he falls and has not another to lift him up!" Nicole and Emilee lifted me up, and together we lifted up the name of Jesus Christ and created resources to encourage other women to do the same. God used their skills to multiply the impact of the ministry. All I had to do was swallow my pride, realize my deep need for community, and ask for help.

The troubling thing is that guilt or pride often gets in the way. At first glance, it seems we would burden someone or perhaps be an annoyance to reach out for help. We may even think we can do it better, faster, or more efficiently on our own. And maybe we can! However, my greatest moments of feeling stuck have happened when I wasn't willing to let go and allow God to use someone else's gifts to advance His kingdom and, in turn, free up my time and resources to have a more balanced life. *Ouch!* I've never said those words out loud before.

Your God-dream might just be between you and God. In that case, I would love to see you really pray and ask God for wisdom about how you could bring someone in to help you, someone who has the gifts and talents you need on your team. You wouldn't believe how much just a few hours a week will help, especially if you're not leaving your nine-to-five anytime soon.

Your Zone of Genius

When we begin building a team, there's a great temptation to hold on to tasks we've grown to love. When I launched my podcast, I was a one-man show. I pitched guests, scheduled interviews, wrote questions, made graphics, managed all post-production tasks, engaged on social media, created show notes … the list goes on and on. When you're just starting out, I think there's some value in being a solopreneur. You learn what it takes to produce your final product. Therefore, when you bring in help, you know exactly what you need.

There comes a sticking point in every leader's life, though, where you can't do it all. There simply are not enough hours in the day. At this point, it's important to find your zone of genius and delegate where you can.

What's your **zone of genius**? As we've firmly established in previous chapters, God has uniquely wired you with the gifts and talents to thrive in your calling. For example, I am a connector and a visionary. I love having conversations on my podcast and setting the vision for what the brand will look and feel like as well as leading my team toward the projects that I feel God would have us work on. Do *I* need to be the one who makes the graphics? No. Do *I* have to write the email campaigns? Nope. Sure don't!

When we delegate tasks that are a drain for us, we will have more bandwidth to thrive where God has gifted us to serve. Revel in the fact that God has wired you to do the things you love. Praise Him for that! Then, think about what it would look like to pass off some tasks to others.

Together is a fun and fulfilling place to be.

In an *Inc.* article, Jim Schleckser explains the 70 percent rule: if someone can do a task to 70 percent as well as you can, you should pass it off if possible.[1] I realize that might feel scary to you, especially if the project is your creation and you've always managed it solo.

> *What if they don't do like I can?* Bad news: they won't.
> *What if it frees me up to do more work in my zone of genius?* Good news: it will.

If you can get over the fear of trusting someone to take on a task, you'll feel such a weight lifted off your shoulders. For me, that looks like allowing interns to pull together biographies, headshots, and other collateral to help me prepare for recordings. I don't make my own graphics anymore. This allows me to use my creative energy to come up with valuable questions, lead conversations that will really matter to my listeners, and engage directly with our online community. It was hard to pass off tasks at first. Now, I often think, *What other areas could I pass off to free up more space in my brain?*

Together is a fun and fulfilling place to be. I don't believe we were meant to win alone. I want to win *with* other people, don't you?

As you work through this phase of your journey, remember that you have brought new members onto your team for a reason. God has gifted them with what you need, and you *need* the help. So train them well and then trust them to do their jobs. Correct where necessary, but remember, the more freedom you give your people, the more freed up you'll be to do the things you're supposed to be sinking your time into. Bottom line: train and trust.

Finding Your Sanity Sisters

While enjoying the season of a new marriage, everything about my life changed in the blink of an eye. All the changes were positive, but they were also difficult.

It was a beautifully hard cocktail of juxtaposition: The blessing of marriage and ministry and the grief of being far from loved ones. The embracing of a new, loving church family and the heartache of leaving deep roots of friendship behind. When small-town Mississippi culture met my Tennessee spitfire and entrepreneurial spirit, I wondered what true community would look like for me.

Invest in co-laborers for the gospel. You won't regret it.

After a year or so, I got to know a few younger women in our church and convinced them to take up running. (I bet you're not surprised.) During the beginning of the COVID-19 pandemic, we would gather at the church and run until we got our sanity back during a time when in-person friendship seemed nearly impossible. One of these women was a stay-at-home momma, navigating her new identity as "Mom." One was a mother of two littles who was considering a business idea to help women organize their homes. The last was a young mom who was finishing up her schooling to become a nurse practitioner. The four of us had nothing and absolutely everything in common. As we ran together, our conversations would range from Jesus to diapers to business ventures.

What these ladies taught me is that we all need **sanity sisters**. Don't tune me out! I'm not at all insinuating that you need to be a runner. I get it. That activity isn't for everyone. However, you do need people around you who will call out your zone of genius, hold you accountable for your actions, and ask about your progress toward your glory goal. We are better when we walk in community with fellow go-getter girls who we are cheering on and vice versa. When we can lean on one another's shoulders, borrow one another's courage, and speak into each situation with genuine love and concern, we are all more effective for the gospel.

To find your sanity sisters, just look around. God is at work within your friends who are starting businesses, building amazing families, and serving your community. They need you and you need them. Be intentional. Invite them to meet you for coffee, and express genuine interest in what God is doing in their lives.

Once you find these peers, keep them! Establish rhythms where you check in or meet in person. Ask how you can pray for one another (and actually do it!). Sometimes it's hard to set aside the time to make these friendships a vital part of your life, but you will get out of the relationship what you put into it. Invest in co-laborers for the gospel. You won't regret it.

Bearing One Another's Burdens

As with many of the principles we've covered in this book, a degree of endurance is required to illuminate the talent around you. The ins and outs of mentorship, the delegation of tasks, and finding the right people to be a part of your ministry or business is hard but holy work. I'm reminded of Paul's letter encouraging the church to carry one another's burdens and not to grow weary of doing good. Let's read Galatians chapter 6 together (and slowly). Think about it in the context of this chapter, and circle words that stand out to you.

> Brothers, if anyone is caught in any transgression, you who are spiritual should restore him in a spirit of gentleness. Keep watch on yourself, lest you too be tempted. Bear one another's burdens, and so fulfill the law of Christ. For if anyone thinks he is something, when he is nothing, he deceives himself. But let each one test his own work, and then his reason to boast will be in himself alone and not in his neighbor. For each will have to bear his own load.

Let the one who is taught the word share all good things with the one who teaches. Do not be deceived: God is not mocked, for whatever one sows, that will he also reap. For the one who sows to his own flesh will from the flesh reap corruption, but the one who sows to the Spirit will from the Spirit reap eternal life. And let us not grow weary of doing good, for in due season we will reap, if we do not give up. So then, as we have opportunity, let us do good to everyone, and especially to those who are of the household of faith. (vv. 1–10)

First, we see a command to **bear one another's burdens**. Let's be the type of leaders who shoulder our team's burdens with prayer and genuine concern. Paul says that in this we "fulfill the law of Christ" (v. 2). What does that mean? When we bear one another's burdens, we are loving one another as He has loved us (see John 13:34–35). To lead in a burden-bearing way will require grit, patience, and a lot of gentleness on our part. We must continually ask God to develop the fruit of the Spirit in us as we love those around us.

Next, Paul gives reminders to the church to **sow seeds in good soil**. This is an important reminder that there will be natural consequences to how we steward our platform and our team (positively or negatively). Again, this is not totally dependent on us in our own strength. We are continually relying on the power of the Holy Spirit in us to give wisdom and discernment. As my husband likes to say:

You will reap what you sow.
You will reap more than you sow.
You will reap in a different season than you sow.

Finally, Paul gives a charge to the church: **do not grow weary in doing good**. We often slap this verse onto mugs and T-shirts without realizing Paul's real encouragement here. He's telling the church to not give up in doing good to others because the good we do has an eternal value, and he wanted us to know that, eventually, we will reap a harvest (even if we must wait to see the fruit in eternity) *as long as* we don't give up.

Lisa Harper extended that kind of grace to me, and I want to model that same type of faith-in-action to others. Don't you? Real community is built in circles, not silos. We may never know the impact on someone's heart when we offer a kind word or a helping hand, but God knows. And God sees.

The Friends Carrying the Mat

In Jesus' ministry, we see Him call His disciples, heal the brokenhearted, and preach to people from all walks of life—not as a religious leader in the temple but as a humble, common man who challenged the religious doctrine of His day (see Philippians 2:5–8). In many stories, He teaches us what it looks like to be a good friend, and in the book of Mark, He shows us how to usher our friends to Himself.

In Mark 2:1–12, we're told that Jesus returned to His hometown, Capernaum, where a large crowd had gathered to see if He really could perform the miracles they'd been hearing about. When a paralyzed citizen learned that Jesus was in town, the man's four friends rallied together to get him to the Messiah in hopes that he could be healed. They arrived at the home to find a rowdy crowd blocking their path. Unable to work their way through the excited onlookers, they took drastic action, carrying their friend up to the roof, where they lowered him down to Jesus. Talk about committed friendship!

When Jesus told the paralyzed man, "Son, your sins are forgiven" (v. 5), the religious leaders were outraged. They accused Christ of blasphemy, insisting that only God could forgive sin. Jesus responded,

> "Why do you question these things in your hearts? ... But that you may know that the Son of Man has authority on earth to forgive sins"—he said to the paralytic—"I say to you, rise, pick up your bed, and go home." (vv. 8, 10–11)

In that moment, Jesus was essentially saying, "I see your heart, and I'm doing this so that you might know Me."

What amazing buddies that paralyzed man had. Because of their assertiveness to get him to Jesus, he was healed and God's true character was shown. What a miracle!

Friend, this is what deep-rooted community looks like in action. Going out of our way to point our people to the Messiah. Reminding them of how we see Him at work through their gifts and talents and the outworking of their glory goals.

Prayer Prompts

Use these prayer prompts to help you pray and journal about what God is revealing to you in this chapter.

God, will You help me:

- illuminate the talent I see around me

- ask for and receive help when I need it

- be kingdom-minded as I approach friendship

FOR THE GO-GETTER GIRL

SCRIPTURE FOR REFLECTION

- Romans 12:4–5
- Ecclesiastes 4:9–10
- Galatians 6:1–10
- John 13:34–35

GOALS

- What is your reaction to the 70 percent rule, and how might you be able to implement it in a way that allows others to shine?

GUMPTION

- Why is it important for us to invest in community? What would it look like for you to do so?

GRACE

- Have you had someone extend grace and kindness to you like Lisa did for me? Who might you be able to extend that same type of help and kindness to right now?

DO THE THING MANIFESTO

Review our manifesto statement for chapters 1–7. Depending on your learning style, you may want to write it down, share it with a friend, or say the words aloud.

I am a go-getter girl for the kingdom of God. I seek to make Jesus Christ known through my work and to live in dependence on Him as I use my gifts and talents.

By the power of the Holy Spirit, I take step after step toward the God-dream He has put in my heart. When I stare at a blank canvas, I'm certain He will give me everything I need to advance the gospel.

I persevere with a stick-to-itiveness that the Enemy cannot interrupt or thwart. I will not make light of what God has called me to do. He has called me to a great work, and I will not stop in the midst of discouragement or distraction.

Most days, my calling will look mundane. I will take small steps each day in a Godward direction.

I will create with an unrushed heart, knowing I am operating out of an overflow of my private relationship with my Creator. Striving can cease when I operate by His agenda.

I hold my plans loosely, relying on God for wisdom and discernment about which assignments should come and go in my life. I will prayerfully follow His lead, wherever and whenever He calls me to go.

As I love and lead others from the deep well of how Christ loves me, I help affirm and shine a light on the gifts and talents of those around me.

Chapter 8

THE TENSION OF TIME

We all get the same number of hours each day. But doesn't it seem like some days last forever while others zip by? How can we redeem the time we have been given? This seems to be the million-dollar question all of us are asking. Our culture supports an entire industry dedicated to helping people manage their time, and yet it still seems so difficult to crack the code. What we really desire is some level of control over our time. We value but often misuse the hours we've been given.

In this chapter, we will redeem the way we think about time, learning to see it as one of those "both-and" issues. We can make time for hard work *and* renewing our minds. We can prioritize time for family *and* friends. We can carve out space for strategy *and* Sabbath. It is not impossible (and it won't be perfect), but it does require something that is nonnegotiable: intentionality.

Intentionality is our goal, not perfection.

In our creative mission, time is our most valuable commodity. Maybe that's why we get a little nervous at the idea of overhauling how we spend it. Like creating a budget to get our finances under control, this adjustment will alter the decisions we make moving forward. When we invite God into an area of our lives and ask Him to transform it, He also transforms *us* in the process. When it comes to time, let's ask Him to be in control of how we spend it.

You Get to Decide

How often do we give our minutes to activities that distract from what God is doing in and around us? How much time do we waste scrolling social media, for example, tapping and comparing as we become spectators to the lives of people we may not even know?

According to a 2020 article in *Digital Marketing*, globally, the average person spends two hours and twenty-four minutes on social media every single day.[1] Let's do the math: 52,560 minutes, 36.5 days, or 876 hours per year. Just the time we spend on social media alone has become a part-time job for all of us, claiming somewhere in the ballpark of sixteen hours of our week! The crazy part? Many of us are willing to let this time go rather than fight to redeem it.

Maybe social media is not your vice. (We could all learn something from you—please email me!) However, I use this common example to make a strong case that we all have an area, whether it be social media or Netflix or time spent sitting in carpool lines, where we can find some minutes (if not hours) to redeem.

Take a close look at your time, and notice any mindless activities that bring you a serotonin hit. How much time are you dedicating to those activities? Could you use that time to work toward your glory goal?

First Corinthians 10:31 commands us: "Whether you eat or drink, or whatever you do, do all to the glory of God." Every minute matters. If His glory is our greatest desire, then we must consider every hour of our day and choose to spend it wisely as we serve Him.

Balance versus Harmony

Let me be the first to say I have always struggled with the concept of a balanced life. When I search the Scriptures, I do not find a great case for balance. I see evidence that we are to practice a regular pattern of rest (see Ex. 20:8–10). I see Jesus' plea to seek His kingdom and righteousness above all things and to not be anxious about tomorrow (see Matt. 6:33–34). But I don't see much about "balance."

When I've been on the search for balance in my life and work, I've often felt like a tightrope walker. Nik Wallenda is a master of the sport, holding nine Guinness World Records for his accomplishments. His most impressive walk was 1,560 feet in the air over suburban Milwaukee, and it took him about thirty minutes to finish the task.[2] I remember sitting on pins and needles watching the television screen as he slowly but surely walked the tightrope, carrying a pole to help him balance his weight. Everything was in check. He meticulously placed his foot on the rope with each step, determination etched on his face. He knew that one misstep could be detrimental (and possibly deadly).

When I strive for balance in my life, sometimes I imagine myself in midair, biceps fatigued from carrying the "pole" in my hands. For a short time, I think I have it all together. But slowly, as I add more and more obligations to my load, my center of gravity shifts, and eventually I grow tired. My imperfections begin to show. My feet grow tired of gripping the tightrope. I become so focused on proving myself that I'm thrown off-balance by trying to carry far more than I can bear.

As God and I sort out how to best manage my time, I've given up on the false promise of balance. Instead, I have come to appreciate a new word: **harmony**. Think about it. When we hear a choir sing, is each member always singing at the exact same tone, pitch, and volume? Probably not. They gather in harmony, delivering a rich depth of beautiful sound. Of course, the melody matters too. This main thread that weaves through a song is the foundation upon which the rest of the song lies. Get the melody wrong and the song follows suit. But when harmonies come beside that melody, *pure magic*!

We must remember the primary melody that threads through our lives: our faith and hope in Jesus Christ.

The same is true of our time. We'll face illnesses, surprises, and shifting priorities as seasons ebb and flow, so we must remember the primary melody that threads through our lives: our faith and hope in Jesus Christ. He is the foundation on which we layer other priorities.

Will each area of our lives fit together into a perfect symphony as we pursue our work? Nope. If we feel burdened to the point where we experience dissonance, harmony may not be possible. It's important that we evaluate opportunities through this lens, asking ourselves two important questions: (1) Does this obligation add to my mission or distract from it? (2) Can I take this on and still maintain *harmony* in this season?

We don't have to walk our tightropes as if our lives depend on it, taking on too much weight and finishing our days exhausted. It's possible for our priorities, work, and relationships to harmonize and create the beautifully layered life that God intended for us.

Intentional Boundaries

We've established that time is our greatest resource and that we must make our minutes matter. Later in this chapter, we will discuss what it looks like to take inventory of how we spend our time, but first we need to tackle another word many of us dislike: *boundaries*.

If I feel tension at the thought of creating a **boundary**, that's a red flag that can indicate the boundary's absence in my life. When I feel the strain or desire to please other people, for example, this is a surefire sign that some guardrails need to be in place for how I think, act, or live. This is true of anything in our lives that lacks discipline and intentionality.

A few months ago, I was spiraling online as various friends posted about their family and career accomplishments. I began to feel like I wasn't progressing quickly enough to keep up. Their baby announcements reminded me that I still wasn't ready to become a mom. Pretty graphics and giveaway posts pushed me to create more content. Their book launches served as reminders that my book was still in the works. It was time for me to draw a boundary and put an end to feeling like I wasn't enough.

Hoping to move in a healthier direction, I established a new guardrail around the time I spent online. I set aside a couple of hours each day, one day each week, and one week each year to stay completely away from social media. I'm still practicing this boundary, and I've found that stepping away from socials helps renew my mind and spark my creativity. I also don't become as subject to groupthink. Instead, I unpack topics I know God is placing on my heart. Often, as a content creator, it's easy to morph into a slightly different version of someone else you see online rather than being the exact you that God has crafted you to become. Time away from our screens helps us have more capacity to dream, cast vision, and create from an authentic place.

Boundaries feel constricting when we have a "fear of missing out" (FOMO), but we must remember that boundaries bring freedom. By saying no, we can align our time with our priorities. By turning down the good, we can find the great.

Chances are you already have pockets of time that need surrendering. We all do. We must listen and obey when God asks us to change how we spend our time in our relationships, with our phones, and in our schedules. Today, let's hold these areas with open hands, praying and believing that God will give us direction in how we spend our time. Freedom comes when we surrender our schedules to God.

If this were easy, I would not be having conversations all the time with women who are still trying to figure it out. It's helpful to realize that most of us are in deep need of rescue from our desire to do everything well and to please every person in our lives.

I never experienced this push and pull as deeply as I did in the season leading up to my wedding. Good intentions I had, but the realities of tying a bow on one chapter of my life while simultaneously uprooting everything I knew made me a complete ball of anxiety. Friends wanted to say goodbye. I had a full-time job that I wanted to finish well while also frantically looking for a new position that would help provide for our family once we moved to Mississippi. I was about to become a pastor's wife, a role I knew nothing about apart from my experience of being raised in the church.

There was so much to do, but all that chaos forced me to maximize my time. I became militant about my schedule in the weeks leading up to our wedding.

I made a list of the people I wanted to spend time with and made plans to see them. I carved out blocks of time to pack and sell my belongings. I set goals at work and wrapped up all the projects before my departure. Every minute counted because I had none to spare. Suddenly I had no time to scroll social media. It was a test of what truly mattered to me (and it was good for my soul!).

Although I would never want to relive that emotional whiplash, I am thankful for what it taught me about how to manage my time. Giving up social media freed up enough space for me to focus on my priorities. You can probably think of a season of life when, because of the stressors you faced, you too had to make changes to keep your priorities, and likely your sanity, in check.

Let me be the first person to give you permission to set boundaries for your time. Search your heart for areas you know will require letting go (for now, maybe not forever). If you are too busy to pursue the glory goal God has put on your heart, then, friend, you are too busy. We make time for what matters most, and nothing should matter more than the call of God in our lives.

Will there be obstacles? Always. Will it be easy? Rarely. Can we hold our lives and our creative missions simultaneously? Yes. However, we must be willing to make hard decisions and set healthy boundaries so that we can manage to do both.

A Creative's Capacity

The greatest determiner of our productivity is our **capacity**. I have both high-capacity and low-capacity friends in my life, and while I identify more with the former, I think it is important that we discuss both as we navigate how to handle our time wisely.

Do you find yourself making lists, creating agendas, and continuing to work on a task even after the clock strikes five? It is likely that you, by default, are a

high-capacity creator. You love order and find joy in crossing tasks off to-do lists. You are not a quitter, and you don't like to leave anything unfinished. This may drive your spouse or roommate nuts, but you are the CEO of your household. A well-oiled machine of tasks and processes mark your work. Others look to you for guidance on how to better manage their work and family.

If any of this sounds familiar, you are also excited about the idea of this chapter because maybe, just maybe, you'll find a hack you can implement in your life. Efficiency is king to you. It trumps any other measure of success: accuracy, complexity, or anything else that might slow you down. Basically, your life motto is "Let's get it done."

If this is you, one of the most helpful pieces of advice I can give is to try to set realistic deadlines. Some people work well under pressure, but most eventually crumble under its weight. It can be helpful to work backward from your deadlines. Start with the end in mind and identify the steps required to get there. Then set realistic goals to complete each of the necessary tasks along the way.

The outcome is His. The obedience is yours.

Give yourself grace when a step takes longer than anticipated. None of us do our best work when we're anxious about finishing a task. My friend Mary Marantz, author of *Dirt*, says, "Slow growth equals strong roots."[3] If something is taking longer than you anticipated, there is likely a reason. Trust God to grow you during the process and bring the right outcome in His own time. The outcome is His. The obedience is yours.

I have a whole slew of friends who fall in the midrange on the capacity spectrum. That might be your story, or you may identify more with the traits of a **low-capacity** work style. In this case, you are not a slave to your calendar. To-do lists are not really your thing. You know the work will always be there, and you have no issue delaying a task or a conversation until the next day. Deadlines feel a tad suffocating to you, but you manage to meet them. You get the work done, even if your path isn't linear. Your life motto is "It'll get done."

While some of your high-capacity friends may wish they were more like you, maybe you sometimes aspire to be more like them. Much like the girl with curly locks pining away for her friend's stick-straight hair, you may admire, if not envy, their diligence and tenacity in how they spend their time.

Let me reassure you: you do not have to "slay the day" like the girl next door. Your proverbial to-do list does not have to be perfectly checked off to find success. What works for another person likely will not work for you. However, it is important that you hold yourself accountable. If structure is not your jam, consider using a planner, scheduling apps, or time trackers to keep yourself moving forward. Just make sure the system isn't overly complicated or you likely won't stick with it.

Think about your capacity in terms of energy levels too. For example, tackle a mentally draining task during the time of day when you have the most brain power. Let's remember the word that has become the through line of this chapter: *intentionality*. Some of you may be excellent at processes and lists. Others may make more space for free flow. The key here is to be who you are so that you can be the creative person God has called you to be.

Time Blocking

One of the most powerful tools I have discovered for managing my time is **time blocking**. I've learned that creating a podcast requires an insane amount of forethought and follow-through. In the beginning, I experienced overwhelm from all the tasks required to produce a finished conversation my listeners would enjoy. Pitching guests, prepping questions, recording and editing interviews, leveling sound, writing promotional copy, and sharing the episode with my audience … it's so much work! No wonder so many podcast hosts experience burnout and nix their shows.

Here is what I know to be true: you picked up this book because you do not want to quit. You desire to be faithful to what God has called you to do. You just need to find the right map and follow it to your glory goal, right?

The first step in time blocking is to **identify any repetitive tasks** and note how often they occur. Do they happen daily? Weekly? Monthly? Apart from the purposes of time blocking, this exercise is also great for identifying places where you spend time on tasks that do not move the needle or that you might be able to delegate to someone else.

Once you have a working list of repetitive tasks, **note how long it takes you to complete these tasks**. For example, I do not enjoy recording intros to my podcasts. I feel like I have to nail the intro in a way that will engage the listener, but I often rerecord them multiple times due to mispronouncing a name or other important information. The intro is only about forty-five seconds long, so if I wrote it ahead of time, I might be able to nail it in two or three takes. By planning ahead, I might complete this task in just a few minutes and make more productive use of my time (while also lowering my frustration levels).

Taking this task a step further (we'll stay with the same example), let's say I produce four episodes per month. If it takes me fifteen minutes to write and record one intro, then I can set aside an hour each month to write and record all four intros at the same time. The stress of doing it in the moment is gone. By preparing what I'm going to say, I'm not scrambling at the last minute to pull this content together.

Do you see the theme here? (Hint: it's called *planning ahead*.)

Your projects or workflows may be different from mine, but I encourage you to take this principle and apply it in a way that helps you. Can you combine similar tasks and set aside time to do them all at once? Where can you find efficiency by being intentional about how you schedule your time?

The last and most important step to successful time blocking is to **remove all foreseeable distractions**. You know what they are. We must become ruthless about eliminating the things that eat our time throughout the day. Put your phone on the other side of the room. Set up an auto-reply for your email, and close the browser. No really, it's a beautiful thing! Most distractions are not emergencies. On average, it takes us twenty-three minutes to refocus when our attention is taken away from what we're working on.[4] I shudder to think of the amount of time I have wasted simply because I entertained distractions that did not matter. If we remove such distractions, then we can eliminate the time we spend throughout the day trying to get back into the flow of our creative work.

Let's make our minutes matter and be more intentional with how we spend each one.

Eternity in Our Hearts

In the Bible, wise King Solomon wrestled with the same fears we experience as we ponder how to spend our time here on earth. In the book of Ecclesiastes, he asked the same question three times within the first three chapters of the book: What gain has the worker from his toil? In other words, he wanted to know if the work we're doing is worth it. Does it really matter?

It should encourage us to know that even this wise leader was aware that our time will ebb and flow depending on what God places in front of us. In

Ecclesiastes 3:1–8, he reminds us that there are times and seasons for different assignments and priorities.

A time to break down.

A time to build up.

A time to seek.

A time to lose.

A time to tear.

A time to sew.

King Solomon says in verse 10, "I have seen the business that God has given to the children of man to be busy with." He then encourages us with a truth that God makes everything beautiful in His timing. Solomon reminds us we were made for eternal purposes. As followers of Christ, we know that what God does endures forever. When we partner with Him, we are living for the eternal.

In earthly terms, we came from dust and to dust we will return. While we are here, let's find harmony in how we spend our time, prioritizing that which will matter in heaven one day. We have the opportunity, as Paul says in Ephesians 5:16, to make "the best use of the time" we have left for the glory of God.

Prayer Prompts

Use these prayer prompts to help you pray and journal about what God is revealing to you in this chapter.

God, will You help me:

- see my time as a gift from You

- seek out better harmony in how I spend my time

- make changes in my schedule that will allow me to serve You more effectively

FOR THE GO-GETTER GIRL

SCRIPTURE FOR REFLECTION

- Ecclesiastes 3
- Ephesians 5:15–17

GOALS

Below, brainstorm areas of your work where you could implement time blocking.

Tasks	Weekly Tasks	Monthly Tasks

GUMPTION

- Read Ecclesiastes 3. How do these reminders about time encourage you?

GRACE

- How can you work toward harmony in how you spend your time? What changes do you need to make to feel more in control of your calendar?

DO THE THING MANIFESTO

Review our manifesto statement for chapters 1–8. Depending on your learning style, you may want to write it down, share it with a friend, or say the words aloud.

I am a go-getter girl for the kingdom of God. I seek to make Jesus Christ known through my work and to live in dependence on Him as I use my gifts and talents.

By the power of the Holy Spirit, I take step after step toward the God-dream He has put in my heart. When I stare at a blank canvas, I'm certain He will give me everything I need to advance the gospel.

I persevere with a stick-to-itiveness that the Enemy cannot interrupt or thwart. I will not make light of what God has called me to do. He has called me to a great work, and I will not stop in the midst of discouragement or distraction.

Most days, my calling will look mundane. I will take small steps each day in a Godward direction.

I will create with an unrushed heart, knowing I am operating out of an overflow of my private relationship with my Creator. Striving can cease when I operate by His agenda.

I hold my plans loosely, relying on God for wisdom and discernment about which assignments should come and go in my life. I will prayerfully follow His lead, wherever and whenever He calls me to go.

As I love and lead others from the deep well of how Christ loves me, I help affirm and shine a light on the gifts and talents of those around me.

As an act of worship to the Author of time, I walk into my days with a steady confidence in my yes and my no, knowing He is at work in me.

VIDEO 4 NOTES (CHAPTERS 7–8)

See the QR code on page 21 for the video link.

Chapter 9

INTERRUPT THE OVERWHELM

Before I married Dustin, I spent my days inside a cold corporate building on the fancy side of town, feeling like the very space I occupied was a prison cell. I had covered my office walls with bright decor and verses that would lead me back to truth anytime I started to lose myself in the toxic work culture. The crazy thing was, I'd really wanted that job. At that point, I had been a corporate recruiter for about five years, and I couldn't think of a better way to serve people than to be a part of their career journey at one of the largest organizations in town.

What felt suffocating was the office politics and the constant worry of "Am I doing enough?" The demands were high, the resources were low, and apart from a few trusted coworkers, it was difficult discern who I could trust. Just pulling into the parking lot made me nauseated most days.

Oddly enough, this season was also one of the most powerful for 818 Ministries. I connected with countless families who were fighting cancer and even used my vacation days to take college students to serve in hospitals, where we impacted thousands of lives.

So I muddled through from eight to five and dreamed of getting home each evening to work on my glory goal. As soon as I burst through the back door of my condo after that long commute, my laptop and belongings would spill across my living room, and I would focus on the ministry until bedtime. There was just so much to do and never enough time to do it all.

Many of you may be experiencing this feeling too. Packed schedules. Increasing responsibilities. A to-do list that never seems to get finished. We know God is on the move, but we sometimes don't know how He's going to work all things together for our good (see Rom. 8:28). It's easy to lose sight of the eternal picture when we sit overwhelmed and frustrated by our daily grind.

Grace is yours for the taking.

As I connect with fellow creators, I see two common themes emerge as a response to overwhelm.

The first is a **head-down mentality**. With this mindset, we keep our heads down, focused on tilling what is hopefully fertile ground as we work without distraction. In this approach, we can't see the forest because we're so busy chopping down trees. We convince ourselves that if we continue working at this pace, then surely the chaos will end soon. When others try to help us, we decline the offer, certain we will finish the task faster if we just do it ourselves. Eventually, exhaustion has its way, and we finally raise the white flag of surrender. Only then do we accept help and move toward a healthier pace of life.

The second response to overwhelm is to become a **vocal energy drain**. With this mindset, we believe that if we can't change our current situation, then we can at least complain about how life isn't fair. As a result, we become exhausted from the negativity and, in turn, so do those who love us. Like a perfectly orchestrated maze of dominoes, this pattern eventually leads to collapse. In this case, we must realize the power of our words. We are commanded in Scripture to "take every thought captive to obey Christ" (2 Cor. 10:5).

The first step to healing is admission. Then, set realistic expectations and practice gratitude; these two key practices will create a paradigm shift from doom and gloom to joy.

You may identify with one of these mindsets. Maybe you have your head down and you're doing the best you can. Or, perhaps, without realizing it, you've dumped your frustration unintentionally on those you most love. Either way, you're not alone. And grace is yours for the taking.

Everything Matters

One of the greatest lessons God has taught me over long seasons of bivocational ministry is that He makes all things matter. He wastes no good thing. He leads us through hard seasons with grace and mercy far beyond our wildest dreams. For example, the years I spent in a corporate recruiter role taught me how to ask really good questions. I didn't see it at the time, but these long days mattered and taught me vital skills I now use as a writer and speaker.

In 1 Corinthians 15, Paul shares with the church at Corinth about the resurrected body and what will happen when Jesus returns. "In the twinkling of an eye,… the trumpet will sound," and death will be "swallowed up in victory" (vv. 52, 54). Wow. What a powerful reminder of what will be ours as children of God on that final day.

Paul then encourages the church to devote themselves fully to the work God has placed before them, saying in verse 58, "Therefore, my beloved brothers, be steadfast, immovable, always abounding in the work of the Lord, knowing that in the Lord your labor is not in vain."

Here, Paul is telling us that nothing God places before us is in vain. He makes all things matter in His kingdom. Therefore, if you are in a difficult season or stuck in a job that doesn't fulfill your greatest passions, heed His encouragement. God will not waste this moment. He is preparing you for what comes next.

God will not waste this moment. He is preparing you for what comes next.

Nonnegotiable Rest

There's a great temptation for a girl like me to give you all the strategies to do the thing while neglecting a vitally important piece in how we live out our calling: rest. I'd love to say it's in my nature to relax, but I bet you can already tell it's not. God and I have been on quite the journey together when it comes to rest, and—while I have not yet arrived—He has taught me a lot over the last few years.

In my years of singleness, I was a complete and total workaholic, finding my identity in a to-do list of "achievements" for God. After all, if I didn't have the thing I longed for the most (marriage), then I assumed the alternative was to work myself to the bone.

Then, after I married Dustin and moved a day's drive away from my Tennessee family, church, and community, I had a choice to make. I could turn to busyness and make achievement my idol once again, or I could rest in the Lord and trust where He had planted my feet in Mississippi.

This is when I learned to value being **fulfilled** more than filling my schedule. It's also when I started to realize that rest can be the fuel that propels us forward.

Have you ever noticed that your strongest ideas come while you're singing in the shower, taking a long walk, or even when you're sleeping? There's a reason why! It's because in the moments of mental rest, our brains can break away from the influx of information that's pounded into them every day.

In a 2012 NPR article about sparking creativity, Sarah Zielinski states, "Sleep helps generate new ideas in several ways. During sleep, the brain consolidates memories. That act of consolidation actually reorganizes thoughts, much like organizing books on a shelf. The new arrangement can help extract knowledge and generate new associations."[1]

Take it from a recovering workaholic: rest is an essential component of our lives. We were designed to crave it, and God provides so much evidence in His Word that it's good for us. When we allow time for God to renew us, we more clearly radiate Him to the world around us.

Recognizing the Signs

We don't have to let overwhelm have the final word. While I am speaking specifically to the go-getter girl experiencing a busy, unruly schedule, I realize some of you may be in a dark season of severe anxiety. If that is you, I wish I could give you a hug and encourage you to seek professional help from a doctor and/or therapist. Advocating for our mental health is just as important as focusing on our physical health.

Often, we hear mixed messages that suggest we can just "pray away" severe anxiety or depression (or that it will go away if we *just trust God more*). Please hear me when I say: I recognize the harm in these kinds of messages and that is *not* my encouragement to you. While I definitely believe prayer and faith are crucial for all of us, I also recognize that God has given us psychological support systems in addition to spiritual ones. Both matter, but for the purposes of this book (and because I'm not a mental health expert), we'll focus our discussion on the spiritual and physical aspect of general overwhelm.

If you are in a season of overwhelm due to a busy schedule or unchecked priorities, you might be experiencing the following symptoms:

- **Baseline overwhelm:** Do you wake up and immediately feel a baseline level of overwhelm that lasts throughout your day? Is it difficult to focus because the sheer volume of work feels too weighty? Do you think, *Maybe if I could just swim to the surface somehow, I might no longer feel like I'm drowning?*
- **Short fuse:** Do you find yourself having a quick temper with your team and/or family, snapping over little things that shouldn't bother you all that much?
- **Negative self-talk:** Do you find yourself stuck in negative thought patterns based in fear or insecurity? Do you often have thoughts that sound like this: *I can't imagine ever getting out from underneath this stress. It feels like it will always be this way!*

First, if you are experiencing a steady stream of overwhelming thoughts throughout your day, I would encourage you to evaluate whether you're facing circumstantial stress or a more serious clinical issue that needs to be addressed by your therapist or doctor.

However, if you feel that your schedule and priorities have simply gone awry, you may find it helpful to refocus your affections on the Lord and remind yourself of three biblical truths:

1. *God is sovereign.* This means He is ruling over every area of your life. He has not forgotten about you, and He has gone ahead of every detail that seems overwhelming from your current view. (see Col. 1:15–23)

2. *I have the mind of Christ.* When we are in Christ, He imparts wisdom to us when we read His Word and when we listen to the Holy Spirit, who is alive in us. We are not left alone to handle overwhelming circumstances. When we walk in communion with God, He leads our steps. (see 1 Cor. 2:6–16)

3. *I get to choose.* We do not have to stay stuck in a loop of negative thought patterns when we are overwhelmed. We have agency to interrupt our thoughts and replace them with biblical truth. (see 2 Cor. 10:5)

Next, if you find yourself having a short fuse around those you love, it's likely that it's time to implement some boundaries and systems for your work (delegate, delegate, delegate!). Give yourself grace when you're struggling. I have no doubt you are doing the best you can. That doesn't mean you can't arm yourself with better ways to do what you're already doing to become a more effective "you."

Last, if you find yourself in a spiral of negative self-talk about your busy lifestyle, it's time to practice interrupting those negative spins. To take your thoughts captive and name what you're feeling or experiencing, you must first acknowledge that your thoughts are doing more harm than good. Then, identify a truth to speak over the lie. This will help you move forward.

For example, let's say you're discouraged because you're unable to spend as much time as you wanted preparing for the book club you wanted to start because you have little ones at home. You could interrupt that thought pattern with this: "My children are a blessing from the Lord. They are not a 'distraction' from my glory goal. Maybe I can start a book club for other moms with young children, offering support to one another while also building friendships for our children." Then, you can walk into your glory goal feeling less overwhelmed and more excited about what God is doing in your current season.

Batch Working

For a friend's birthday many years ago, we visited a waterpark resort called Wilderness at the Smokies. One of the slides required riders to sit on an inner tube and then enter the water flow at the top of a large bowl. Once inside the giant vortex, there was no escaping. Round and round you went until it finally sucked you down the central shoot and shot you out into a large pool at the bottom of the slide.

Sometimes, our overwhelm feels like being in that waterslide. We go round and round, scared half to death, and we wonder if we'll ever find our way out again.

To me, being trapped inside the swirly, enclosed bowl of the slide felt suffocating, as do days when I feel overwhelmed with no way out. In these times, we must remember to turn our gaze upward, with eyes on heaven, expectant for how God will work in our lives. We listen, surrender to His plan, and trust that we'll land exactly where we're meant to be in the end (even if we have to hold our breath on the way through it).

I find that in seasons of overwhelm, sometimes what I need isn't more time but a better system.

Sometimes it's not what we do but how we do it that makes us feel overwhelmed.

What do I mean by this? Well, many times we can be doing all the "right" things but in an inefficient way, so we end up wasting our valuable time and adding unneeded stress to our days.

For example, I might feel overwhelmed when I think about cooking for the week. But when I take some time to map out a meal plan, schedule a grocery pickup, and prep ingredients, I'm amazed at how much less stressed I feel at dinnertime each evening. I also gain mental clarity out the wazoo because I no longer have to worry about what I'm going to fix. This is the very same reason Steve Jobs wore the same black turtleneck to work every day. Any small decision that we can eliminate from our days frees up creativity for other endeavors.

I find that in seasons of overwhelm, sometimes what I need isn't more time but a better system. One of the most helpful ways I save time is through batch working.

Batch working is a way of organizing tasks into groups and then completing similar or repetitive tasks together. For example, if you know a particular day of the week is going to be busy, blocking time for tasks like laundry or cleaning will help your brain rest because it creates a flow to help your household run more smoothly.

This method of organizing my life has helped me free up mental space in my work life too. Because I have developed efficient batch systems, I'm less overwhelmed. Batch working allows me more time and energy to put toward my glory goals and opens me up to more life-giving activities. Even just a couple of tasks batched together could save you a ton of time over the long haul.

Be a Steward

I recently had a conversation with my husband about a situation that had been frustrating me. Despite countless prayers and deep faith, God had not moved in the way I was hoping. Dustin quickly reminded me that I was responding to God's inactivity (at least in my mind) by stomping my feet and trying to change the situation myself. Ever been there?

"Rebecca," he reminded me. "As growing disciples of Christ, we must follow where He leads. He knows what's best for us and will direct us in the way that will bring Him the most glory and us the most good."

Dang. Gut punch right there. As a go-getter girl, I instinctually want to take the reins, find a solution, and make sure it's okay with God before I move forward. With big decisions, my yes means "yes" and my no means "no." So if I'm in, you'd best believe I am *all the way in*. However, if I don't operate at God's pace, I can easily run ahead of Him and miss what He is doing right in front of me. In this particular conversation, I was fighting the urge to "fix" something God had laid before me instead of receiving that specific situation as a blessing from Him.

Do you realize that the opportunities in front of you are God-given? He led you to the exact place where you are right now and is at work within you. If you believe this, then you have to believe that your work is a gift from Him too. He gave it, He sustains it, and He is faithful to walk with you through it.

Many times we act like the CEO of our lives rather than the steward of a God-given calling. I say "we" because I am the chief of sinners! When we truly partner with God in the assignment He has placed before us, it feels more natural to come to Him for discernment when we feel angsty about what's next. This requires us to believe that God is sovereign and in total control of our lives. All we have to do is follow His lead.

Let It Be to Me

Sometimes we're in a season that takes us completely and totally by surprise, like the COVID-19 global pandemic. Something happens in the world and, suddenly, life as we know it shifts. In the Gospels, we see Mary, the mother of Jesus, encounter a life-changing (dare I say overwhelming?) moment that altered the course of eternity. Our lives, even now, are marked because of what God did through her willing response to overwhelming news (see Luke 1–2).

How could it be that *this* was God's best for her? Having been a faithful fiancée to her betrothed, Joseph, imagine the fear and confusion she must have felt upon learning she was with child. The overwhelm might've overtaken her, as she wondered how in the world she would mother the Savior of the world.

When Gabriel told her the news, he said, "The Holy Spirit will come upon you, and the power of the Most High will overshadow you; therefore the child to be born will be called holy—the Son of God. And behold, your relative Elizabeth in her old age has also conceived a son, and this is the sixth month with her who was called barren. For nothing will be impossible with God" (Luke 1:35–37).

Did you read that? *Nothing is impossible with God.* Mary's response to Gabriel was beautiful and full of faith. She said, "Behold, I am the servant of the Lord; let it be to me according to your word" (v. 38).

What a response full of confident hope in who God is and who He created her to be. We can follow Mary's example and accept God's directives by saying, "Let it be to me. Whatever is best for Your ultimate plan and purposes." (And yes, Elizabeth, who had been barren, did in fact conceive, as God said she would.)

As we walk into seasons of overwhelm, we can remember that, ultimately, God makes all things matter. Just like Mary, we do not get to see behind the curtain into how He is weaving our stories into the overall tapestry of the redemption of creation. But we can stand with the same confidence Mary did, no matter our circumstances.

Prayer Prompts

Use these prayer prompts to help you pray and journal about what God is revealing to you in this chapter.

God, will You help me:

- set aside time to create rhythms of rest

- recognize overwhelming thoughts and replace them with Your truth

- remember that You make all things matter

FOR THE GO-GETTER GIRL

SCRIPTURE FOR REFLECTION

- 1 Corinthians 15:58
- Ephesians 3:20
- Luke 1–2

GOALS

- Where might you be able to use batch working to help increase productivity and decrease overwhelm?

GUMPTION

- Do you currently operate more as a CEO or a steward of your life? What would it look like to begin to shift your mindset toward stewarding the life you've been given?

GRACE

Did you relate to any of the signs of overwhelm? What is a negative thought pattern you are currently experiencing? Practice interrupting that thought and replacing it with truth by using the pattern below.

DO THE THING MANIFESTO

Review our manifesto statement for chapters 1–9. Depending on your learning style, you may want to write it down, share it with a friend, or say the words aloud.

I am a go-getter girl for the kingdom of God. I seek to make Jesus Christ known through my work and to live in dependence on Him as I use my gifts and talents.

By the power of the Holy Spirit, I take step after step toward the God-dream He has put in my heart. When I stare at a blank canvas, I'm certain He will give me everything I need to advance the gospel.

I persevere with a stick-to-itiveness that the Enemy cannot interrupt or thwart. I will not make light of what God has called me to do. He has called me to a great work, and I will not stop in the midst of discouragement or distraction.

Most days, my calling will look mundane. I will take small steps each day in a Godward direction.

I will create with an unrushed heart, knowing I am operating out of an overflow of my private relationship with my Creator. Striving can cease when I operate by His agenda.

I hold my plans loosely, relying on God for wisdom and discernment about which assignments should come and go in my life. I will prayerfully follow His lead, wherever and whenever He calls me to go.

As I love and lead others from the deep well of how Christ loves me, I help affirm and shine a light on the gifts and talents of those around me.

As an act of worship to the Author of time, I walk into my days with a steady confidence in my yes and my no, knowing He is at work in me.

I am simply a steward of the life God has placed before me. I do not bow a knee to the effects of overwhelm. I take my cues from heaven, and God is my sure foundation.

Chapter 10

SILENCE THE CRITIC

Right before Dustin proposed to me, Mom and I took a girls' day to shop in our natural habitat, Hobby Lobby. (To paraphrase the Grinch: "Then she got an idea! An awful idea! The Grinch got a wonderful, awful idea!")[1] It probably won't surprise you to hear that I had a wild hair to surprise Dustin with a painting. I'd decided to spotlight a waterfall from the Smoky Mountains, a location that had come to mean a lot to us. At this point, we had selected an engagement ring, and I had a feeling this would be the spot where, in the coming months, he would propose. (Spoiler alert: I was right!)

I scurried through the aisles in the Hob Lob (as Mom and I lovingly call it) to find the canvas, paint, and brushes I would need to begin my masterpiece. Then I rushed back to my parents' home and set up my supplies in their living room. As I sat at the card table, still marked with paint from my childhood, Mom looked at Dad with a very familiar smile and said, "She's got a vision."

This is a phrase that has been used often by my parents throughout my life. I've always been an visionary kind of gal. (In middle school, I launched a jewelry-making business with my best friend because Girl Scout cookies were too "copy/paste" for a girl like me.) Every time I started to do something out-of-the-box creative, my parents would look at each other and say, "She's got a vision!"

On this particular day, I looked up from my blank canvas and said, "Yep, I do!"

With a look of concern, Mom studied the waterfall picture on my phone. I looked at her and said, "I just don't know if I can do it."

But I was certainly willing to give it my best shot. For hours, and then days, I painted and I painted and I painted. At times, I almost threw that painting in the trash, and at one point the waterfall looked more like cotton candy than water. I couldn't seem to get it right, and the more I painted, the more I doubted that I would ever finish this gift for Dustin. Each time I felt like giving up, I would take a few deep breaths, determined to clear all thoughts of *I can't do this* swirling around my mind. Then I'd come back to the canvas to keep chipping away at it, one brushstroke at a time. It took me multiple weekends to finish the job, but lo and behold, *I did it*. And you know what? Dustin loved it!

That "She's got a vision" statement that my parents always say, sort of tongue-in-cheek, really means, "We're not sure how she's going to do this, but we know she will." I'm sure glad they believe in me, because a lot of times I struggle to believe in myself. It's not that I'll throw in the towel; I'll just often get caught in thought patterns that aren't encouraging my progress.

Maybe you've been there too? Feeling that you have the vision of what God is asking you to do but just not sure how you'll get there. We must begin to see our uncertainty as an opportunity to exercise faith. Our inner critic is full of lies. And as we learn to silence her, God's truth will ring louder and louder in our minds.

Upside-Down Confidence

When it comes to confidence, we as women can find it particularly challenging to maintain a biblical perspective. We think, and many times we're told, that if we keep telling ourselves we're accomplished enough, or pretty enough, or good enough … *then* our inner critic will finally go sit in a corner (goodness, I wish she would). In reality, a feel-good affirmation will never penetrate our hearts enough to silence our inner critic. We must interrupt negative thought patterns and replace them with God's truth (for encouragement, read Philippians 3).

While we indeed do not have it all together, we serve a sovereign God who does.

We have an active role to play in seeing ourselves the way Christ sees us and living in light of His redemptive promises. When we decide that the Enemy no longer gets to boss our thoughts, we can step into a place of true kingdom-based confidence, where we rightfully belong. This is not a false message that we have it all together. Instead, it's a steady knowing that while we indeed do not have it all together, we serve a sovereign God who does.

Our worth and identity rest in the finished work of Jesus Christ on the cross. Nothing more is needed, nothing less will do, and nothing (and no one) else will ever satisfy our hungry, weary souls. Try flipping your confidence upside down for a change. Finding certainty in who we are in Christ is the first and most important step toward silencing the lies of the Enemy and walking with confidence into our God assignments.

What do I mean by lies of the Enemy? See if any of these statements sound familiar to you:

- *I'm not good enough.*
- *This is too much for me.*
- *I am too much for them.*
- *She's doing that better than I can.*

These are just a few examples of discouraging thoughts. To retrain our minds and silence our inner critic, we are going to take ourselves through a **thought-life inventory** based on a verse nestled in Philippians 4.

Here, Paul has just spoken to the church at Philippi about anxiety and how the peace of God guards our hearts (see Phil. 4:7). He then shares a list of qualities that should mark our thoughts. He says, "Finally, brothers, whatever is true, whatever is honorable, whatever is just, whatever is pure, whatever is lovely, whatever is commendable, if there is any excellence, if there is anything worthy of praise, think about these things" (v. 8).

Let's take ourselves through two lists of questions based on this verse. When you catch yourself having negative thoughts, ask yourself these questions:

- Is it true?
- Is it honorable?
- Is it just?
- Is it pure?
- Is it lovely?
- Is it commendable?
- Is it excellent?
- Is it worthy of praise?

Now, if we stopped there, we would probably find that our thoughts are not in alignment with God's. However, if we don't move past that realization, it's likely we'll drift back to negative thinking. To fully turn from our inner critic toward godly thoughts, we must ask ourselves another set of questions:

- What is true?
- What is honorable?
- What is just?
- What is pure?
- What is lovely?
- What is commendable?
- What is excellent?
- What is worthy of praise?

Just as we can combat overwhelm by taking our thoughts captive, we can silence our inner critic by reframing our thoughts in a Godward direction instead of letting the Enemy slow us down.

He Lives in Us

God used a moment at the end of my first full marathon to impress this idea of kingdom-based confidence in me. Many months of training had led me to a big pink "START" sign as my whole body shivered in the cool morning breeze. I was running the Donna Marathon in Jacksonville, Florida, a charity event that supports breast cancer research. This was one of the most meaningful days of my life because Mom was going through chemotherapy treatments at the time. I had a lump in my throat as the national anthem was sung. When the gun went off and pink confetti flew into the air, the feeling as I hit Go on my watch was surreal. That day, I would run 26.2 miles for the first time, each step a physical representation of my dreams to support patients fighting a similar battle to the one my mom was facing. The entire experience felt weighty and holy and good.

It was about fifty degrees with not a cloud in the sky when, at mile 18, I began to feel the effects of running fifteen to twenty seconds per mile faster than my coach had instructed. My legs had become heavy cinder blocks, hurting more deeply with each stride. Even though I was hot, my body kept shivering because of the wind. *The wall.* It was real, and very quickly I began to wonder if I would ever see the finish line. *Had I trained enough? Would I have to quit? What if I let myself down?*

While texting my dad an update, I finally crossed the 20-mile marker. I had come so far, but I still had so far to go (6.2 miles to be exact). Isn't that a lot like how we feel about our glory goal at times? We take step after step of obedience, but the voices in our head begin to discourage and distract us, making us weary of the journey.

At mile 25, I remembered I had saved a song on my playlist for this point in my race. The song "Yahweh" from Elevation Worship played as I gazed out over the most beautiful view of Jacksonville. While descending the bridge, I got overcome as the song reached the end.

> *He who was and is to come*
> *Is the one who lives in us.*
> *The Great I Am*
> *Yahweh.[2]*

Through those lyrics, God was reminding me that He was giving me the strength and grit to persevere. Relying on Him, I approached the 26-mile marker. As soon as I spotted the finish time clock, I gunned it, finishing strong with a smile on my face—four hours, twenty-four minutes, and thirty-seven seconds. As a volunteer put a medal around my neck, I don't think she had any idea of the significance of that moment. I had silenced my inner critic and conquered fatigue, pain, fears … all to cross that finish line as a reminder that there was hope for Mom. I couldn't control cancer—nor could I save her life—but I could run that race as a declaration of my faith over fear, showing the world that I trusted God not just to see me across the finish line but to see my mother back to good health if it was His will.

Can I encourage you to take that next step, remembering that the Great I AM is with you? Choose to conquer that spiral of negative thoughts and to agree with how God sees you instead.

Decision Paralysis

If you've planned a wedding, even the simplest wedding, you know it requires no less than 1.2 million decisions. (I'm only half-kidding.) When Dustin and I got engaged, I swore I would not be "that bride" who cared about every little detail. However, while I hope I wasn't a bridezilla, I did care deeply about a few things. Mainly, I saw our wedding as a big opportunity for our closest loved ones to hear the gospel. We both have friends who very openly don't have a relationship with the Lord, and we knew they would be present for our special day (a huge opportunity that we didn't take lightly).

We thought about this chance to represent God to our loved ones as we planned our ceremony. We thought about it as we wrote our vows and ceremony and selected songs and prayer warriors. We wanted everyone to leave the ceremony having heard the gospel and clearly seen a picture of our faith. That was the glory goal. That was what mattered most to us.

Of course, it required dozens of small decisions to reach that end. For example, I remember sitting on the couch, shopping online for plastic dinnerware for the reception. You would imagine it would be sold in sets of logical numbers. However, like hot dogs and their buns, some of the dinnerware I liked had to be combined in different quantities until I had what I needed. I spent about an hour trying to do the math before I finally thought, *This is ridiculous. I will never get this hour of my life back that I have spent looking at plastic cutlery.*

This is a great example of **decision paralysis**. You may laugh at my cutlery story, but let's not pretend we don't do this on a regular basis in our work. We each face endless opportunities when it's tempting to dwell on something that doesn't really matter. Does cutlery matter to the extent that we needed to provide utensils for our guests at the reception? Yes, but it certainly wasn't something to lose sleep over.

Colossians 3:1–2 tells us, "If then you have been raised with Christ, seek the things that are above, where Christ is, seated at the right hand of God. Set your minds on things that are above, not on things that are on earth."

Even while seeking things that are above, we will have to make difficult decisions. However, we can focus on the eternal and not spend unnecessary time on the trivial.

Maybe you're setting up your Etsy shop and you need to select shipping supplies. Perhaps you oversee the craft for women's night at your church and you've been frustrated because you can't find the perfect project. Maybe you want to host a Bible study but you're worried about how your house looks when people come over.

When you start slipping into analysis paralysis, keep the main thing the main thing and spend the majority of your time making decisions that will lead to that end. If you find yourself drowning in decisions, take a step back and remind yourself of the glory goal.

Not-So-Perfect Timing

If there's one thing this current season of life is teaching me, it's that most things worth pursuing are never going to feel convenient or comfortable. As I'm writing this chapter, Dustin and I have been married for about two and a half years. I've experienced more change in these few years than I probably have in the rest of my years combined.

Once Dustin and I began to feel a little bit settled in Mississippi, a new rental home became available. Everything about it made sense. It would give us more room and even grant us a backyard for our dog. However, we would have to paint every square inch of the house to make it our own.

I was excited about how perfect the rental was for us but also overwhelmed by how much work it would be to paint it. Plus, we were leaving in less than a month for a nine-day trip to the Holy Land, and we'd have to decide within the next few days if we wanted the lease. Daring to take the leap, we said yes, and I immediately went to Home Depot to buy paint.

Hoping to divide and conquer, we decided that I'd paint and Dustin would handle the move. The work was hard, inconvenient, and frustrating. During the worst moments, we doubted we'd made the right decision. But now that we're a couple of years past that transition, I'm incredibly thankful we did it. My home office setup is more efficient, we now have plenty of storage space, and we're just overall super thankful for a home we can enjoy as a family and share with the people we love.

Now, could we see all that in the thick of the transition? Absolutely not. The stress could have overwhelmed us and stopped us from seeing the blessing we were being given.

Instead, we kept our heads down and focused on the end goal. We had faith that if we kept going where God was leading us, He'd have something good in store for us on the other side. And we were right.

If you find yourself doubting a decision or facing an inconvenience, take a deep breath and remember that you're in a temporary transition. As you face each choice, ask yourself:

- Will this help me pursue my glory goals? *In this case, yes. The new rental would give us more space to host people, offer me a better place to work, and provide a more relaxing home for us to rest in.*
- Does it make sense financially? *The house fit our budget.*
- In ninety days will I be glad I did this? *I knew if we could get through the initial move and painting, we'd be a lot happier. And we are!*

Next time you are second-guessing your not-so-perfect timing or doubting your decisions, remember that perfection doesn't exist. Rather, seek what is profitable. God will give you the grace, favor, and energy for the decision that will most honor and glorify Him.

A Man of Valor in the Winepress

One of the best scriptural examples of God's response to someone doubting their calling is the story of Gideon. Let's take a field trip to Judges 6 and walk through this passage.

The Israelites had done "evil in the sight of the LORD, and the LORD gave them into the hand of Midian seven years" (v. 1). After being invaded and oppressed by the Midianites for years, the angel of the Lord appeared to Gideon, who was hiding from the Midianites. Notice the powerful truths shown in this exchange between Gideon and the angel of the Lord.

> And the angel of the LORD appeared to him and said to him, "The LORD is with you, O mighty man of valor."
>
> And Gideon said to him, "Please, my lord, if the LORD is with us, why then has all this happened to us? And where are all his wonderful deeds that our fathers recounted to us, saying, 'Did not the LORD bring us up from Egypt?' But now the LORD has forsaken us and given us into the hand of Midian."
>
> And the LORD turned to him and said, "Go in this might of yours and save Israel from the hand of Midian; do not I send you?"
>
> And he said to him, "Please, Lord, how can I save Israel? Behold, my clan is the weakest in Manasseh, and I am the least in my father's house."
>
> And the LORD said to him, "But I will be with you, and you shall strike the Midianites as one man."
>
> And he said to him, "If now I have found favor in your eyes, then show me a sign that it is you who speak with me. Please do not depart from here until I come to you and bring out my present and set it before you."
>
> And he said, "I will stay till you return." (vv. 12–18)

Let's break this down. First, God reminds Gideon that He is with him. How comforting is that? No matter what happens, no matter how bad it gets, no matter if we fall on our faces in defeat, *He will never leave us.* In the face of doubt, that promise keeps us going and brings us comfort.

God is never too busy or rushed to tend to your heart's cry when you're struggling. He is faithful to answer your hard questions with His unchanging truth. The best thing about that? God isn't intimidated by your hard questions. Remember, He already knows what you're going to say before you even utter a word. He also has the answers. Our response to His leading says a lot about the condition of our hearts.

God is never too busy or rushed to tend to your heart's cry when you're struggling.

Next, God calls Gideon by a name that probably felt a little bit intimidating to Gideon. The angel calls him a "mighty man of valor," a phrase that can also mean "mighty warrior." There he is, hiding from the Midianites in his wine-press, and now God's calling him *a mighty warrior*? That had to feel a little off to Gideon. However, in Scripture, God often calls unlikely people.

God is famous for using the *unusable*. We see this play out again and again in the Bible. Gideon was hiding in fear when God called him to defeat the Midianites. David was a shepherd boy armed with nothing but a slingshot and stones when God called him to defeat the giant. Peter often spoke without thinking but was called to be one of Jesus' disciples. Moses stuttered but was called to speak to Pharaoh and lead his people out of slavery. Rahab was a Gentile prostitute who was called to save the Israelites. Jonah was a coward who was called to save Nineveh. Mary was a teenage virgin when she learned she was carrying God's child. Goodness, Jesus Himself was born in a lowly Bethlehem barn and grew up in Nazareth (not the best neighborhood of His day—see John 1:46).

Yes, God is in the business of equipping extremely ordinary people to do extraordinary things in His name. As my husband, Dustin, says, **"If God will appoint you to it, He will equip you for it."**

After God calls Gideon a "mighty man of valor," Gideon questions Him. If I were in his shoes, I would probably have done the same. Gideon feels as if he and the Israelites have been forsaken, and he can't understand how he is supposed to be the one to save them from the hands of the Midianites. Gideon basically says, "If you're really with me, then I need you to prove it to me!"

Chapter 6 goes on to show how God humors Gideon's request for a series of miracles.

In the first one, Gideon prepares a young goat and unleavened cakes. God has him put them on a rock and pour broth over them. Fire springs up from the rock and consumes the meat and loaves. In return, Gideon builds an altar there and calls it "The LORD Is Peace" (v. 24).

In the second miracle, Gideon tells God that he's going to lay a fleece of wool on dry ground. If the fleece has dew on it the next morning, he explains, then he'll know God will save Israel by his hand. When Gideon checks the next morning, the fleece is so full of dew that when he wrings it out, the water fills up an entire bowl. As if this isn't proof enough that God is who He says He is and is the Promise Keeper, Gideon asks God to do the reverse. Proving His power yet again, God leaves dew on the ground while the fleece remains completely dry.

Chapter 7 moves on to talk about how God whittles down Gideon's army from thirty-two thousand to three hundred men. This scares Gideon. How is he supposed to defeat the Midianites with just three hundred men? Daring to move forward in faith, Gideon and his men approach the camp, blow their trumpets, and smash jars in their hands. The Lord sets the sword of every

Midianite soldier against his comrade, meaning, He makes them fight against themselves!

What makes me want to stand up and cheer when reading this story is that Gideon didn't get an ounce of the glory. God did. God didn't strategically build up an army with the technical skills needed to succeed, although He could have. He didn't multiply Gideon's army to be so large that the mere size of it alone would guarantee victory over the Midianites, although He could've done that too. Instead, He decided, "Gideon, I'm going to whittle down your army until it's so small, you have no other option but to trust Me, My plan, and My power. Now watch Me!"

> # Life is too short and eternity too long to have our eyes on anything or anyone but Him.

Sometimes God whittles down our armies too. Don't let that make you doubt Him. When you take a step of obedience, everyone isn't going to come alongside you. Don't let that delay your step of faith, but instead, let God's prompting propel you forward. Please don't succumb to someone else's opinion when God has already spoken. Take the step of faith, and keep your eyes on Jesus. Life is too short and eternity too long to have our eyes on anything or anyone but Him.

Prayer Prompts

Use these prayer prompts to help you pray and journal about what God is revealing to you in this chapter.

God, will You help me:

- take my thoughts captive when they stray from Your truth

- act boldly, knowing You are my foundation

- trust Your timing

FOR THE GO-GETTER GIRL

SCRIPTURE FOR REFLECTION

- Judges 6
- 2 Corinthians 2:15

GOALS

- In what area is God prompting you to see your confidence through a more kingdom-minded perspective?

GUMPTION

Let's practice interrupting our inner critic with truth. Take some time to ask yourself our questions from Philippians 4:

What is true?

What is honorable?

What is just?

What is pure?

What is lovely?

What is commendable?

What is excellent?

What is worthy of praise?

GRACE

• Are you frustrated by the timing of how things are moving forward? Talk to God about your worries, and trust that His timing is best.

DO THE THING MANIFESTO

Review our manifesto statement for chapters 1–10. Depending on your learning style, you may want to write it down, share it with a friend, or say the words aloud.

I am a go-getter girl for the kingdom of God. I seek to make Jesus Christ known through my work and to live in dependence on Him as I use my gifts and talents.

By the power of the Holy Spirit, I take step after step toward the God-dream He has put in my heart. When I stare at a blank canvas, I'm certain He will give me everything I need to advance the gospel.

I persevere with a stick-to-itiveness that the Enemy cannot interrupt or thwart. I will not make light of what God has called me to do. He has called me to a great work, and I will not stop in the midst of discouragement or distraction.

Most days, my calling will look mundane. I will take small steps each day in a Godward direction.

I will create with an unrushed heart, knowing I am operating out of an overflow of my private relationship with my Creator. Striving can cease when I operate by His agenda.

I hold my plans loosely, relying on God for wisdom and discernment about which assignments should come and go in my life. I will prayerfully follow His lead, wherever and whenever He calls me to go.

As I love and lead others from the deep well of how Christ loves me, I help affirm and shine a light on the gifts and talents of those around me.

As an act of worship to the Author of time, I walk into my days with a steady confidence in my yes and my no, knowing He is at work in me.

I am simply a steward of the life God has placed before me. I do not bow a knee to the effects of overwhelm. I take my cues from heaven, and God is my sure foundation.

I have an unshakable kingdom-based confidence in who God made me to be and how I show up in the world to make Him known this side of heaven.

VIDEO 5 NOTES (CHAPTERS 9–10)

See the QR code on page 21 for the video link.

Chapter 11

LAY DOWN THE MEASURING STICK

My feet stumbled as I climbed aboard the StairMaster at the gym. I held my feet in place while situating my phone and water bottle in their respective holders, wondering how it would be possible to take a sip of water without falling. I held tightly onto the armrests as the stairs began to move. *This isn't so bad.* About the time my feet had found their groove and my workout playlist had pumped me up, a woman climbed onto the machine next to me. Misery loves company, they say, and I appreciated the presence of another human subjecting themself to this kind of torture.

But then my competitive nature kicked in, and what had originally felt like company turned into a full-on Olympic competition. Without the woman noticing, I glanced to see what she had set her speed to and slowly increased my machine to match hers. One click at a time, I exceeded what she was doing. Out of breath, I continued climbing and climbing. After sixty seconds or so, lactic acid built up and my legs burned, warning me that in my quest to measure up, I was only exhausting myself. All I wanted was to match, and hopefully exceed, what StairMaster girl beside me was doing. Was that too much to ask?

Click by click I reduced the speed to where I had started, and my heart rate eased back to a healthy range. The woman beside me was none the wiser about what was happening; she was engulfed in her Kindle book. I, however, was completely embarrassed and reminded of my propensity to compare and compete (even with just myself). Can you relate?

From a young age, we learn that measuring tools are used to determine success and failure. Standardized testing marks our ability to pass from one grade to the next. Stopwatches count how fast we run a mile in gym class. There are many more necessary but nevertheless daunting places in our lives where we are measured. This conditioning teaches us to strive for a lower number on the scale, a higher score on the test, a more completed to-do list, and a faster time in the race. That's not always a bad thing. It's good to acknowledge when we are improving, growing, and learning. But when we enter adulthood, we rarely loosen our grip on that ruler.

It can be tempting to observe others, our eyes seething with comparison. She got a promotion. Her engagement ring was bigger. She got to quit her full-time job and go all in with her business before me. Her Instagram hit 10K followers before mine. We spend our days attempting to measure up to other people, completely missing God's purpose for us right here and right now. What if there's a better way?

Have You Not Heard?

When we are steeped in comparison and our senses focus on areas of disappointment, consumerism, or envy, we hinder our ability to be effective stewards of our gifts. I admit: I am the chief of comparison and competition. After moments of envy, I often leave Instagram and think I can do it all. I feel completely unstoppable … until I am stopped. Contrary to what our sky-high motivation would have us believe, we are not bulletproof. Even in the tasks and work we are most passionate about, we all have limits.

The theological truth that we often forsake here is that God is infinite. He has no limits. *None.* He is the author of time, and He will never tire or feel rushed by someone else's agenda.

The prophet Isaiah tells us all about this characteristic of God when he says:

> Have you not known? Have you not heard?
> The LORD is the everlasting God,
>   the Creator of the ends of the earth.
> He does not faint or grow weary;
>   his understanding is unsearchable.
> He gives power to the faint,
>   and to him who has no might he increases strength.
> Even youths shall faint and be weary,
>   and young men shall fall exhausted;
> but they who wait for the LORD shall renew their strength;
>   they shall mount up with wings like eagles;
> they shall run and not be weary;
>   they shall walk and not faint. (40:28–31)

Sometimes, I get so lost in my own competitive drive that I need a friend to look me square in the eyes and, with the zeal of Isaiah, say to me, *"Have you not known? Have you not heard?"*

The truth is, when we have zero might, God gives us strength. Why? Because He is limitless and we are not. It's not a work-by-our-own-hands kind of strength but one that, as followers of Christ, allows God to enter into our weaknesses, empower us by His strength, and enable us to walk into the world with a confidence that no measuring stick could ever give us.

Our work is more effective, our ministry is more powerful, and our lives are filled with more abundance when we are living in the truth that we have limits but the God who is working in and through us does not.

You Are Not a Clone

When I began speaking and teaching the Bible, I had the best intentions. I wanted women to know God, believe what His Word says about them, and live out what He has placed inside their hearts. However, I struggled with major anxiety before I would speak. On the day of an event, I would watch speakers I admired and try to emulate their styles and prayers.

Shortly after I married Dustin, I was invited to speak at a women's worship night. Thrilled at the opportunity to share God's Word, I got to work. I polished my message and practiced how my transitions would flow. The day of the event, I spent several hours watching many of my favorite Bible teachers: Lisa Harper, Lisa Bevere, and Priscilla Shirer, just to name a few. As I did, I picked up on several nuances and phrases that I particularly enjoyed. Man, could Priscilla pray the house down. Lisa Harper injected humor into her messages in a way that lowered people's defenses. Lisa Bevere spoke with such conviction that listeners couldn't help but lean in close.

When I stepped onstage, having pulled a quote from Priscilla's prayer, I prayed. I delivered my message with as much gusto and passion as I knew how, red lipstick and armpit sweat to prove it. When I left, I felt disappointed in myself but couldn't put my finger on why. People were so kind and receptive, and I felt God had moved hearts, but why wasn't I pleased?

A few weeks later I admitted to my husband, "I think I'm trying to clone my favorite speakers … create a meshed-together style and call it my own."

Dustin got teary as he said, "Rebecca, you're approaching this all wrong. I remember when I, too, did the exact same thing with my preaching style early on. I can't wait for you to step into your own voice. I think the world needs to hear it."

I cried too.

God has wired each of us with unique gifts and a voice that He wants us to use.

In our creative work, it's easy to slip into a pattern of trying to be the clone of someone we admire. But this doesn't benefit us or the people we're trying to serve. God has wired each of us with unique gifts and a voice that He wants us to use. He has placed each of us within a community to serve with excellence. When we try to become someone we're not, it distracts us from how we can be usable for the kingdom.

Imagine if Giacometti had tried to emulate the sculptures of Michelangelo or if Celine Dion tried to sing like Dolly Parton. When you are the "you" that God intended, you will excel at the work God has placed in your heart. Your style, your words, your creativity—all for His glory. You are not a clone of anyone. You are a unique masterpiece, crafted by a God who knows exactly what He's doing.

Our Greatest Distraction

A mild case of panic struck me when I scrolled my Instagram feed; comparison stopped me dead in my tracks. *She got the thing I want.* The next step was happening for her before it happened for me. *What if I had worked harder to grow my platform? Would I have reached this stage more quickly?* My thoughts ran wild as I seethed with envy. My intentions, I thought, were pure, but somehow I couldn't escape feeling like I had been left out, looked over, or passed by.

Most of us have had these moments; we just don't like being honest about them. It's not our best look, so we try to stuff our thoughts about comparison into a box we label "Things I'm Not Supposed to Experience as a Christian." We know we are "enough" in Christ, but why does that sometimes *not feel enough* for us?

First, **we know way too much**. At our fingertips, we have access to absolutely everything that is going on in the world. Do I love social media and think it's an incredible tool for the gospel? Absolutely. Do I also believe it can be the greatest contribution to our demise if we let it consume us? Absolutely. We must begin to see social media as a tool for our ministry and not allow it to discourage our souls. When we spend hours a day on a device that reminds us how our lives and careers don't look like "theirs," it's no wonder we become exhausted and beat down.

Kingdom values are different from the world's idea of success. The world cares more about *accolades* than *honor*. It cares more about *status* than leading with *a servant's heart*. God wanted to make sure Samuel was aware that He sees things differently as the prophet searched for the next king of Israel. Before many of Jesse's sons were brought before Samuel, the Lord said, "Do not look on his appearance or on the height of his stature, because I have rejected him. For the LORD sees not as man sees: man looks on the outward appearance, but the LORD looks on the heart" (1 Sam. 16:7).

Then, a young man came in from working the fields. David, the unexpected one, was anointed to be king that day. His eligibility for kingdom use had nothing to do with his age, stature, or social standing. *He was God's man for that job.*

And he was anointed long before he became king, which is a lesson we would all do well to remember as we patiently seek after God's best for us. David's season of kingship was preceded by many years of faithfulness (for further study, read 1 Samuel 16:1–13).

When we have no guardrails erected around our online lives, our souls feel starved for satisfaction and success from a worldly perspective. We have to saturate our minds with God's truth in order to drown out the noise.

> # Let's celebrate the work He's doing in other people's lives while trusting He is also at work in ours.

Second, **when we find ourselves stuck in comparison, we are often not honoring our season**. We may see a new baby, a career move, a new business venture, or a new book deal and think we are behind. We combine the successes from everyone's highlight reels together into a composite of what we feel we need to achieve. When we focus on what God has seemingly *not* placed in our lives, we dishonor the work He *is* doing within us. Maybe the season isn't what you expected. That doesn't mean "she" is further along than you are. What helps us truly honor our season is gratitude for what God has put right in front of us.

If I'm honest, there are times I wish I lived in closer proximity to people in my industry. I spend most of my business days alone, typing away behind my desk. Most of my recording is done virtually, and most days my work can feel lonely. If I lived somewhere like Nashville, Charlotte, or Colorado Springs, I would be closer in proximity to many friends and I would get to be a part of what they're doing. Have you ever felt that FOMO?

When FOMO starts to get the best of me, I exhale and remember that God has placed me exactly where I am for a reason, blessing this season with friendships I treasure, work that I'm passionate about, and a community I've come to love. What this season lacks in recreation or fun, it makes up for in allowing me space to create. And so I accept my current season as a both-and. It's both boring (at times) *and* productive. It's isolating *and* wildly fulfilling.

I bet you have your own version of a both-and story. I want you to honor whatever it is that God has placed in front of you. Allow your gratitude to grow, and let bitterness and envy be starved of their gumption. God is always moving on our behalf, whether we are aware of it or not. So let's celebrate the work He's doing in other people's lives while trusting He is also at work in ours.

What It's Time For

My friend Jeanette asked me to be on her podcast, *It's Time for Coffee*. When we got to the end of our recording together, she asked me a really important question: "Rebecca, what is it time for in your life?"

My chin rested in my palm and my mind spun as I struggled to answer her question. At that point, I was really battling comparison, as many industry friends seemed to have things happening for them at a faster rate than I did. Book deals left and right. Speaking engagements galore. While I didn't say anything particularly poignant on Jeanette's podcast, I have remembered the question.

It brings clarity, doesn't it? When we identify what it's time for in our lives, *what it's not time for* becomes abundantly clear. What doesn't matter fades off into the distance. It's there. *Oh yes*, it's there and we're aware of it, but it doesn't own us to the degree it did before. We are about our Father's business, and we understand what He's put in front of us to steward right now.

Celebrating Your Limits

The great news is that God has us here, doing this work, for a specific purpose. We don't have to concern ourselves with the sneaky appeal of comparison because He has a race marked out for us that is unique and just for us (see Heb. 12:1).

Instead of being frustrated by our limits and our areas of weakness, what if we celebrated our limits? Limits allow us to lean on God and His strength as our primary source of fuel. They remind us that we are nothing without Him and that He is faithful to meet us in the places of our greatest lack. Every day is an opportunity to realize on a deeper level just how dependent we are on Him. When we stand in confidence—not in who we are but in who He is in us—it's much easier to stop comparison at the door and appreciate that He is empowering us by His Spirit to do the things only we can do.

> ## Limits allow us to lean on God and His strength as our primary source of fuel.

As we celebrate our limits and invite God's strength to peek through our weaknesses, we may find places we need to set boundaries. Here are three helpful sentences we can use when we're caught in the spin of comparison.

I'll get to that tomorrow. Sometimes, we are running at a pace that feels unsustainable simply because we love our work and don't want to push something to the next day. When we can identify what has to be done today versus what can happen this week or this month, we can confidently delay a task or project. When we close a tab in our brains, we can focus with a deeper concentration on the work we need to accomplish today.

I need help. For many of us, this might be the hardest statement. Admitting we need help does not mean we are failing. It means we are admitting that we, unlike God, have limits. We want to bring other people into our work so we can accomplish our God-assignments "as for the Lord," rather than for ourselves (Col. 3:23).

I will aim to finish this by _____. Sometimes we overestimate or underestimate how long it will take us to complete something or how taxing it will be for us. When I started writing this book, I set a goal of writing one thousand words each session. (That lasted about a week.) I have learned to give myself more grace and to work at a pace that allows me to hear direction from God along the way. Can you give yourself a soft deadline but also the grace to tackle the work as the inspiration or time allows? This type of workflow feels less rigid and more sustainable long-term.

The Least Likely of Women

In a world where a woman's highest calling was bearing a son to carry on the family's legacy, Judah's daughter-in-law, Tamar, disguised herself as a prostitute and slept with her father-in-law in desperation. She bore him twin sons and named one of them Perez. Her story was messy and broken and yet still redeemable (see Gen. 38). What Tamar didn't know at the time was that Perez would eventually be in the lineage of the Messiah. She wasn't the only unlikely one to be included.

Unlike Tamar, who pretended to be a prostitute, Rahab was a Canaanite prostitute from Jericho. She bravely answered God's call and offered shelter to Israelite spies, putting herself in harm's way to do kingdom work (for the full story, read Josh. 2). Eventually, she married into the tribe of Judah and gave birth to Boaz. Rahab is another powerful reminder of how God uses the unusable for His purposes.

Unlike Tamar and Rahab, Ruth (the Moabite widow we discussed earlier in the book) had a fierce loyalty to family. In her efforts to care for her mother-in-law, Naomi, she met Boaz, whom she would later marry, and she gave birth to Obed. Obed was also in Jesus' lineage, showing how God redeemed Ruth's story and used her life to pave the way for the coming of His Son, Jesus. (Consider reading her full redemption story in the book of Ruth. It's a quick read.)

Of all these women, Bathsheba was simply in the wrong place at the wrong time (see 2 Sam. 11:1–4). David saw her bathing on the rooftop, and, as she was not allowed in her culture to refuse his advances, an affair ensued. As a result, Bathsheba gave birth to (King) Solomon, David's heir. He was a precursor to the coming of the expected One—Jesus. Again, we see the story of His coming unfolding through the least likely people.

Finally, as we've discussed, Mary was an unwed teenage virgin who was told by the angel Gabriel that she was carrying the Messiah (see Luke 1:26–38). As you think about these scenes from Scripture that led to the coming of Jesus, it levels the playing field quite a bit, doesn't it? It disarms our tendency to assume that Jesus' coming wasn't messy or broken. In fact, it was very messy and quite broken.

It should fill our hearts with hope to know that we can lock arms with our fellow sisters in Christ and celebrate the place our lives hold in the overall story of redemption. You have a role to play in it.

Prayer Prompts

Use these prayer prompts to help you pray and journal about what God is revealing to you in this chapter.

God, will You help me:

- remember that I have limits and You don't

- recognize areas of comparison

- stay focused on the assignment You've placed before me

FOR THE GO-GETTER GIRL

SCRIPTURE FOR REFLECTION

- Isaiah 40:28–31
- 1 Samuel 16:1–13

GOALS

Use the following space to identify what it's time for and what it's not time for in your current season.

What It's Time For	What It's *Not* Time For

GUMPTION

- Have you had an experience like I had that day at the gym, pushing yourself beyond your limits to compete with someone else? In what areas do you feel exhausted from the comparison game today?

GRACE

- How does it encourage you to know that God does not have limits? What would it look like to live like you believe God is infinite and you are finite?

DO THE THING MANIFESTO

Review our manifesto statement for chapters 1–11. Depending on your learning style, you may want to write it down, share it with a friend, or say the words aloud.

I am a go-getter girl for the kingdom of God. I seek to make Jesus Christ known through my work and to live in dependence on Him as I use my gifts and talents.

By the power of the Holy Spirit, I take step after step toward the God-dream He has put in my heart. When I stare at a blank canvas, I'm certain He will give me everything I need to advance the gospel.

I persevere with a stick-to-itiveness that the Enemy cannot interrupt or thwart. I will not make light of what God has called me to do. He has called me to a great work, and I will not stop in the midst of discouragement or distraction.

Most days, my calling will look mundane. I will take small steps each day in a Godward direction.

I will create with an unrushed heart, knowing I am operating out of an overflow of my private relationship with my Creator. Striving can cease when I operate by His agenda.

I hold my plans loosely, relying on God for wisdom and discernment about which assignments should come and go in my life. I will prayerfully follow His lead, wherever and whenever He calls me to go.

As I love and lead others from the deep well of how Christ loves me, I help affirm and shine a light on the gifts and talents of those around me.

As an act of worship to the Author of time, I walk into my days with a steady confidence in my yes and my no, knowing He is at work in me.

I am simply a steward of the life God has placed before me. I do not bow a knee to the effects of overwhelm. I take my cues from heaven, and God is my sure foundation.

I have an unshakable kingdom-based confidence in who God made me to be and how I show up in the world to make Him known this side of heaven.

I am confident that God has planted my feet firmly, in this season, for a purpose far greater than I can imagine. Rather than getting caught up in comparison, I will allow Him to do what only He can do in and through me.

Chapter 12

FALL IN LOVE WITH YOUR LANE

One day, I opened my inbox to find an email I'll never forget. It was from a sweet momma of three who lives in central Texas. We have similar hearts, interview many of the same people on our podcasts, and had followed each other for a while. In fear of being too similar and wondering if she would even want to be my friend, I had neglected to reach out to her first. My heart leaped as I saw the subject line. *Podcast Guest.* Here is a taste of the beginning of our friendship:

Hey Rebecca!!!

I am so pumped to be connecting with you! I LOVE following along with you on Instagram, and I feel like we are destined to be friends!! I really loved your end-of-year book season. We have SO many loved books in common! I love that!! Also I just need to say that you are KILLING the reels game!! The winter one made me laugh so hard … #tryingNOTtofreezeintexas.

I am Jeanette Tapley and I love all things friendship, laughter, and a good cup of coffee. I am a wife, a mom to teens, an author, a speaker and, like you, a podcaster! I host the *It's Time for Coffee* podcast, where for the past 3 years I have met with friends weekly to talk about life, faith, and friendship. It's my heart and goal with my podcast that our friends and listeners would feel heard, valued, and never alone, no matter what stage of life they find themselves in.

I would love to join you on your show, *Do the Thing Movement*, to talk about friendship! My heart is to meet each friend right where they are, and the opportunity to do so on your show would mean the world to me! I'm just your pal Jeanette here to encourage you and your listeners.

Thanks so much for considering me as a guest on your podcast. I look forward to connecting about this opportunity soon!

Your friend,

Jeanette[1]

I read the email again and looked around my empty office. This felt so different from previous encounters with women in my industry. It felt like Jeanette knew her lane and mine, and there wasn't, for once, a feeling of scarcity. She hadn't asked to "pick my brain," (code for "Can I easily learn what *you* learned the hard way?"), and it seemed she truly wanted to collaborate. She celebrated my lane, and I instantly wanted to do the same for her. Long story short, Jeanette became the friend I didn't know I needed.

Now, she's someone I deeply trust when it comes to processing big decisions, asking hard questions, and (maybe most importantly) celebrating big and small wins. Nothing is really off the table for us. She FaceTimed me the day she got the link sticker on Instagram. She was the first person I saw after I signed my book deal because she happened to be driving through our town. We also frequently celebrate the wins we have in podcasting that others might not understand or care about.

I'm telling you this because falling in love with our own lane allows us to cheer loudly for others, be confident in our work, and celebrate wins and losses with others (even those in our industry). However, from personal experience, I know that feeling confident in the work God has called us to do is not easy, especially in a world where we compare likes, progress, or success at every turn.

The first step to falling in love with your lane is identifying it. In chapter 1, we established how your God-given gifts and talents intersect with you building God's kingdom. The more we remind ourselves of these truths, the more clarity we will have around what is our lane (and what is not).

Next, we must remind ourselves of God's sovereignty (His power, or what I sometimes like to call His "in-control-ness"). In our limitations, we often forget that the same God who parted the Red Sea and partnered with Elijah to defeat the prophets of Baal is actively working in and through our lives. Where He has us now and the assignments He's placed before us are gifts of grace from His hand.

In Ephesians 1:11, Paul says, "In him we have obtained an inheritance, having been predestined according to the purpose of him who works all things according to the counsel of his will." God knows the plans He has set forth for us. They are in agreement with His will for our lives. He works things together for good for those who are called according to His purposes (see Rom. 8:28). That's you and me, sister!

Someone else's win should never be treated as a personal loss for us.

When we are abundantly clear on what our lane is and we remind ourselves of the truth of God's sovereignty, **then, and only then, can we cheer loudly for the people around us**. I dare even say that we can do so unhindered by envy and full of joy for how God is at work *in them*. Someone gets a promotion? Cheer loudly, knowing God has placed each of you right where He wants you. Someone else moves into the home you've long been admiring? Cheer loudly, remembering that longing and celebration can coexist. Someone else's win should never be treated as a personal loss for us.

Next, we have to make sure we don't skip over our own wins. Self-deprecation is a skill I learned from an early age. (In the southern Bible Belt, the line between true humility and making ourselves feel small so the other person won't be intimidated is very blurry.) If we want to thrive in our gifts, we have to live in awareness of how God is at work in and through us. For me, I have a celebration crew—an army of friends who care about my work and genuinely want to celebrate with me.

Bottom line: you need one too. Not so you can boast or be prideful but so you can own what God is doing around you with people who know your challenges and offer a safe space for you to share.

Who are the people in your life that run alongside you, cheering you on instead of trying to take over your lane?

Authentically You

Just as we can get caught in the comparison trap, it's easy to let insecurity prey on our minds. When I was launching my podcast, I feared I might not have the personality to carry a show. I said this out loud to a friend, who said, "Rebecca, you just need to be fully you, and your work will fall into the laps of the people who need it."

Friend, the same is true for you. As we've established, your calling, your God-given talent, and your assignment were all God's good idea. He knows your challenges. He knows your anxieties. He knows your fears associated with what He's called you to do.

Hebrews 12:1–2 tells us, "Therefore, since we are surrounded by so great a cloud of witnesses, let us also lay aside every weight, and sin which clings so closely, and let us run with endurance the race that is set before us, looking to Jesus, the founder and perfecter of our faith, who for the joy that was set before him endured the cross, despising the shame, and is seated at the right hand of the throne of God."

> # When we are authentically ourselves, we find freedom to unapologetically glorify God in a unique way. And in the process, we give other people permission to do the same.

The author and perfecter of our faith is also the author and perfecter of our time here on earth. Therefore, where He has placed you—the decisions He's placed on your heart, the shoes He gave you to fill—is all yours. When we are authentically ourselves, we find freedom to unapologetically glorify God in a unique way. And in the process, we give other people permission to do the same.

It's not your job to become like so-and-so. That's not what living a life of obedience to Christ looks like. We fix our eyes on Jesus, the one seated at the right hand of the throne of God, take our cues from Him, and run in the lane He has called us to run in. Not her lane or his lane—our lane. That way, and only that way, will we find the people God meant for us to serve.

He Holds the Pen

Colossians 1 says,

> He is the image of the invisible God, the firstborn of all creation. For by him all things were created, in heaven and on earth, visible and invisible, whether thrones or dominions or rulers or authorities—all things were created through him and for him. And he is before all things, and in him all things hold together. And he is the head of the body, the church. He is the beginning, the firstborn from the dead, that in everything he might be preeminent. For in him all the fullness of God was pleased to dwell, and through him to reconcile to himself all things, whether on earth or in heaven, making peace by the blood of his cross. (vv. 15–20)

He is before all things, and in Him all things hold together. God crafted you in such a way that in serving Him, you would have much joy, glorify Him, and go forth to spread the gospel.

In Him all things hold together. He is the glue that holds together your gifts, your skills, your imperfections, and your fears in a collage of goodness, so you can walk into the world, despite its challenges, full of faith that He will use you for the good of others and His glory.

Friend, He holds the pen to your life. And, trust me, He is a brilliant author. Like any good story, yours will be filled with twists and turns you didn't expect. He is penning something gorgeous through your obedience. Continue to hone your craft and become the best, most God-honoring "you" that you can possibly be.

He holds the pen to your life. And, trust me, He is a brilliant author.

No Doesn't Mean Forever

I sat in a hardback chair, clueless as to what was about to happen. Fingers clasped, I tapped my foot and read over my presentation one last time before my name was called. The writing conference I was attending gave writers the opportunity to pitch a book idea to a literary agent or an acquisitions editor at a major publishing house. It was *Shark Tank* style with only fifteen minutes to share your idea and hear their thoughts.

In sixty seconds or less, depending on how quickly I talked, I would concisely share my idea and save the rest of the time to listen. I believed I had the best book proposal the world had ever seen. Surely, they would see my passion and desire for this project and want to work with me, out of all the women they would meet with that day.

"Rebecca!" the conference volunteer exclaimed as she came out to get me. I wiped my sweaty palms on my professional dark-wash jeans and readied myself to meet the agent. I told her about my idea, and she patiently listened. Graciously she gave me some actionable feedback about how I could hone my craft and package the book I wanted to write.

I left encouraged. The next day I had a similar appointment with an editor for a publishing house whose work I deeply admired. We had a similar conversation to the one I'd had with the agent. The feedback was unanimous. It was a no—*for now.* The eternal optimist in me was hopeful about the feedback they had given me, but at the same time, I left feeling defeated and deflated.

Rejection's sting can discourage us at times, especially if we feel we are truly partnering with God on a new adventure. Sometimes, rejection is an indicator that we need to go in another direction.

In this case, God used the conference to redirect my efforts toward a future project that would be the best it could possibly be. If I had left holding only their opinion of my proposal, too discouraged to press into the hard, refining work that became my next steps, you wouldn't be holding this book in your hands today.

Let's face it: We all experience the sting of rejection at times. It's easy to feel like others are holding our dreams in their hands. They stand at the gate and control what happens next, or so it seems.

By now you know I love a good story. Not all of them have a Cinderella ending, as we've all lived long enough to learn. There's not always a perfectly tied bow after each sting of rejection.

However, after that conference, I did put in the work to refine my message, build an audience who wanted to hear from me, and draft a new book proposal in pursuit of a traditional publishing deal.

The very same agent, Blythe Daniel, and the same publishing house, David C Cook, that had rejected me in the beginning became the partners that, seven years later, are walking alongside me now to get this message into your hands. God had to have looked down and winked during those moments at the writing conference when I wondered if my dream of writing would ever come true. I had no idea what was coming; neither did they.

A *no for now* does not mean a *no forever.*

The Ultimate Call

Throughout this book, we have discovered many stories in Scripture that have given color to how we can pursue our gifts and talents to honor God. We've seen some major and some minor characters, although all of them were used by God to accomplish His agenda of redemption and restoration that is still in play today. Ultimately, the true hero within all these pages is Jesus Christ. He left His throne in heaven to dwell among us, took on flesh, and experienced the temptations we face as humans, yet without sin (see Heb. 4:15).

His earthly ministry was filled with moments that turned the heads of religious leaders. Ultimately, His thirty-three years of ministry on earth were headed toward an expected end. He was rejected, betrayed, tried, beaten, and crucified as payment for our sins (see Luke 22–23). He endured unspeakable suffering on our behalf, and we now have the invitation to be restored to God by placing our faith in Him (see Eph. 2:1–10).

If you have never made that decision, may I encourage you that today is the day of salvation (2 Cor. 6:2)?

If you have, what a joy it is to live out the unique expression of how God has gifted you to bring glory to Himself. May we always see our time and talents in light of the gospel, and may we live and serve as the co-laborers with Christ that He fashioned us to be!

Prayer Prompts

Use these prayer prompts to help you pray and journal about what God is revealing to you in this chapter.

God, will You help me:

• have the wisdom to know what my lane is

• remember that "no for now" doesn't always mean "no forever"

• remember that You hold the pen of my story

FOR THE GO-GETTER GIRL

SCRIPTURE FOR REFLECTION

- Ephesians 1:11
- Hebrews 12:1–2
- 1 Peter 2:9
- 2 Corinthians 2:15–17
- Colossians 1:15–20
- Exodus 3:7–10

GOALS

- Are you running in your lane right now? How would you define your lane?

GUMPTION

- Do you find yourself struggling to believe what God says to be true about you? Whose beliefs are wrong—yours or God's?

GRACE

- Read Ephesians 1. Make a list of what God says about you. How does this encourage you to persevere in your glory goals?

DO THE THING MANIFESTO

Review the full "Do the Thing Manifesto." Let's read these words together one last time. Depending on your learning style, you may want to write it down, share it with a friend, or say the words aloud.

I am a go-getter girl for the kingdom of God. I seek to make Jesus Christ known through my work and to live in dependence on Him as I use my gifts and talents.

By the power of the Holy Spirit, I take step after step toward the God-dream He has put in my heart. When I stare at a blank canvas, I'm certain He will give me everything I need to advance the gospel.

I persevere with a stick-to-itiveness that the Enemy cannot interrupt or thwart. I will not make light of what God has called me to do. He has called me to a great work, and I will not stop in the midst of discouragement or distraction.

Most days, my calling will look mundane. I will take small steps each day in a Godward direction.

I will create with an unrushed heart, knowing I am operating out of an overflow of my private relationship with my Creator. Striving can cease when I operate by His agenda.

I hold my plans loosely, relying on God for wisdom and discernment about which assignments should come and go in my life. I will prayerfully follow His lead, wherever and whenever He calls me to go.

As I love and lead others from the deep well of how Christ loves me, I help affirm and shine a light on the gifts and talents of those around me.

As an act of worship to the Author of time, I walk into my days with a steady confidence in my yes and my no, knowing He is at work in me.

I am simply a steward of the life God has placed before me. I do not bow a knee to the effects of overwhelm. I take my cues from heaven, and God is my sure foundation.

I have an unshakable kingdom-based confidence in who God made me to be and how I show up in the world to make Him known this side of heaven.

I am confident that God has planted my feet firmly, in this season, for a purpose far greater than I can imagine. Rather than getting caught up in comparison, I will allow Him to do what only He can do in and through me.

God has carved out a lane just for me in His kingdom. I run with my gaze fixed on Him. He holds the pen to my life and, boy, is He a brilliant author.

VIDEO 6 NOTES (CHAPTERS 11–12)

See the QR code on page 21 for the video link.

HERE'S WHAT I HOPE

As we conclude our time together, I hope you're standing a little taller than you were when you opened this book. My prayer is that in these pages you've discovered a lot about our God and a lot about yourself.

I hope you …

- have the truth you need to take the next step, even if it feels shaky
- trust God as He asks you to start, endure, or even quit a "thing"
- see your time as a priceless gift from God
- take the opportunity to cheer with joy for the people around you
- keep your eyes on Jesus instead of comparing yourself to others
- live like you know the Holy Spirit is taking up residence inside you
- give all you've got to use your gifts and talents to the glory of God

I'm cheering for you (like, really loud). Let's go, girls!

Rebecca George

ACKNOWLEDGMENTS

God, thank You for rescuing me from my sin through Jesus, redeeming me, applying Your righteousness to my life, and adopting me as Your kid. Evermore, I will love You. Evermore, I will serve You. Thank You for opening the door for this dream to come true.

Dustin, you are my greatest cheerleader (publicly and privately). You point me to Jesus always. You've dried my tears, hugged me tight, and encouraged me throughout every day of this process. Your leadership is all over the pages of this book. I hope you see it. I love you more than I ever have and the least I ever will.

Mom, you believed this day would come (even when I doubted). You and Dad helped me save up to go to my first writing conference even when you wouldn't see your ROI for many years to come. Your relentless determination for *me* to see what *you* see in me helped me to not quit all these years. I got my spunky personality and my desire to encourage others from you. I wouldn't have it any other way.

Dad, you taught me what it looks like to pursue what matters most. Whether it was being an amazing dad, teaching a Sunday school class, or running a marathon, you never gave up, and I get my dogged perseverance from watching yours. You are wildly consistent yet fun. Firm in what will last and easygoing about what won't. Thank you for always being proud to be my daddy.

Blythe Daniel, my literary momma. I am so blessed to call you my agent. I dreamed of working with you since the day I nervously shook your hand and pitched you my idea at She Speaks in 2015. You make aspiring authors' dreams come true with both the grit and the grace that an amazing agent requires. A million thank-yous would never repay the investment you've made in me.

Susan, thank you for giving this first-time author a chance at her dream. You believed in the message God put on my heart, and your initial yes began a ripple that resulted in this book that you hold in your hands. I'm forever grateful that my publishing journey started with you.

Julie, your editorial eye is what made this book shine. Thank you for making my first experience working with an editor one to be coveted by other authors. Thank you for caring deeply about maintaining my voice while guiding the reader on a clear path as the book progresses. I'm forever thankful for everything I learned from you.

David C Cook and Esther Press, what a dream to work with you. In the current climate, I couldn't feel more reassured that I'm partnering with a publishing house that is staying true to historic Christian principles. Thank you for offering me a seat at your table.

Jeanette, Rachael, Elizabeth, Nicole, Natalia, Somer, Jodie, Mary, Abby: you get it. You have prayed, laughed, cried, and rallied harder than a friend could ask for. The true definition of community over competition. I love each of you big, and I'm grateful to run alongside you in the writing community.

Reader, ultimately this book is about you. I kept you in mind as I wrote and edited and mulled over every word. I pray it encourages, edifies, and equips you for the work of the ministry. In Jesus' name!

NOTES

Chapter 1: Heaven on Our Hearts

1. A. W. Tozer, *The Purpose of Man: Designed to Worship*, ed. and comp. James L. Snyder (Bloomington, MN: Bethany House, 2009), 23–24.

2. "King of My Heart," on Bethel Music, *Starlight (Live)*, Bethel Music, 2017.

3. Martin Luther King Jr., "What Is Your Life's Blueprint?" quoted in *Seattle Times*, accessed June 13, 2022, https://projects.seattletimes.com/mlk/words -blueprint.html.

4. Tozer, *Purpose of Man*, 28.

5. "Evermore," on Jason Breland, *Believe (Live)*, Hosanna! Music, 2003.

Chapter 3: Spirit-Led Stick-to-itiveness

1. *Merriam-Webster*, s.v. "stick-to-itiveness," accessed September 19, 2021, www.merriam-webster.com/dictionary/stick-to-itiveness.

2. Alli Worthington, "The Incredible Thing That Happened When I Put God and Google Together," Fox News, January 23, 2018, www.foxnews.com/opinion /the-incredible-thing-that-happened-when-i-put-god-and-google-together.

Chapter 4: Own the Ordinary

1. *We Bought a Zoo*, directed by Cameron Crowe (Los Angeles: Twentieth Century Fox, 2011).

Chapter 6: The Invitation to a Finished Work

1. "One in Three Americans Have a Side Hustle," Zapier, January 14, 2021, https://zapier.com/blog/side-hustle-report/.

Chapter 7: Illuminate the Talent around You

1. Jim Schleckser, "When to Delegate? Try the 70 Percent Rule," *Inc.*, August 14, 2014, www.inc.com/jim-schleckser/the-70-rule-when-to-delegate.html.

Chapter 8: The Tension of Time

1. Gary Henderson, "How Much Time Does the Average Person Spend on Social Media?," DigitalMarketing.org, August 24, 2020, www.digitalmarketing. org/blog/how-much-time-does-the-average-person-spend-on-social-media.

2. Brandon Griggs, "Nik Wallenda Makes Longest Wire Walk Ever," CNN, August 12, 2015, www.cnn.com/2015/08/12/entertainment/nik-wallenda -wire-walk-wisconsin-feat.

3. Mary Marantz, "On Striving to be 'Enough': Why Purpose Is Far More Important than Popularity with Sadie Robertson Huff," February 15, 2022, in *The Mary Marantz Show*, podcast, MP3 audio, 00:06, podcasts.apple.com /us/podcast/on-striving-to-be-enough-why-purpose-is-far-more-important /id1478272407?i=1000551146426.

4. Stacey Lastoe, "This Is Nuts: It Takes Nearly 30 Minutes to Refocus After You Get Distracted," The Muse, June 19, 2020, www.themuse.com/advice /this-is-nuts-it-takes-nearly-30-minutes-to-refocus-after-you-get-distracted.

Chapter 9: Interrupt the Overwhelm

1. Sarah Zielinski, "5 Ways to Spark Your Creativity," NPR, June 21, 2012, www.npr.org/2012/06/21/155369663/5-ways-to-spark-your-creativity.

Chapter 10: Silence the Critic

1. *How the Grinch Stole Christmas*, directed by Chuck Jones and Ben Washam (Burbank, CA: Warner Bros, 1966).

2. "Yahweh," on Elevation Worship, *Here as in Heaven*, Elevation Worship, 2016.

Chapter 12: Fall in Love with Your Lane

1. Jeanette Tapley, email message to author, February 15, 2021.

with Rebecca George

r a d i c a l
RADIANCE

Join Rebecca George for a conversation each week that will help us see more clearly what it looks like to radiate the heart of Jesus in all we do. Buckle up, because she'll gather her favorite old and new friends to share inspirational stories, strategic advice, and hard-won wisdom.

To dive deeper, check out these episodes by searching for **Radical Radiance** in your favorite podcast player today!

Episode 131 "Win at Work and Succeed at Life" with Megan Hyatt Miller
Episode 135 "Intimacy with God in Prayer" with Kyle DiRoberts
Episode 136 "Show Up When You Want to Shut Down" with Lisa Whittle
Episode 138 "Fighting Comparison with Contentment" with Alyssa Bethke
Episode 140 "Let God Be Enough" with Erica Wiggenhorn
Episode 144 "Focus on What Matters Most" with Michelle Myers and Somer Phoebus
Episode 148 "Redeeming Your Time" with Jordan Raynor
Episode 159 "Serving in Jesus' Name" with Wess Stafford
Episode 185 Joni Eareckson Tada
Episode 224 "Trade Striving for Grace-Based Effort" with Kaitlin Garrison

Connect with Rebecca at **radicalradiance.live**